The Memory Endures

The Author as a young man

The Memory Endures

Reg Curtis

*The Story of a Grenadier Guardsman and
Pioneer of The Parachute Regiment
1937-1945*

BY THE SAME AUTHOR

Churchill's Volunteer

Tafelberg

First published in the UK in 2014 by Pilots Publishing, Canterbury CT4 5PE

This edition August 2020
Reprinted March 2021
Reprinted September 2021

ISBN: 978 0 9932053 1 6

All profits in respect of this book are donated to Support Our Paras, The
Parachute Regiment and Airborne Forces Charity

Dedication

I dedicate this book to
all my Airborne friends who
never came back, whose
actions made it possible
for me and other Airborne
friends to enjoy over
seventy years living.

TO BETTY FRANCES

Who helped me so much.

And to former members of the 1st Battalion of
The Parachute Regiment.

Contents

Foreword

by Stephen Cooper, Chief Executive, Support Our Paras, The Parachute Regiment and Airborne Forces Charity

It is an honour to be invited to write the Foreword for this new edition of *The Memory Endures* by Reg Curtis.

On behalf of Support Our Paras, The Parachute Regiment and Airborne Forces Charity, I would like to thank our veteran Reg for his service and for his steadfast loyalty.

Reg was there at the creation: he volunteered in 1940 and was one of the founding members of 1st Parachute Battalion; he fought in North Africa, where 1st Parachute Brigade earned the name 'Red Devils'; he fought in Sicily. He was shot and lost a leg at Arnhem.

Reg never forgot his comrades. He dedicated this book to "all my Airborne friends who never came back, whose actions made it possible for me and other Airborne friends to enjoy over seventy years living".

For the rest of his life Reg stayed in touch with his surviving brothers in arms and at the time of his death it is believed that he was the last man standing from the original 1940 volunteers who called themselves No. 2 Commando, 11th SAS, 1st Parachute Battalion.

Before he passed away in January 2016, Reg pledged income from this book to our charity. It was his wish to support soldiers who may be experiencing circumstances similar to his own, following the amputation of his right leg after the Battle of Arnhem. We are deeply grateful.

Reg's family continues this support in his memory, with all profits kindly pledged in perpetuity. We extend our most sincere thanks to them also.

Reg, we salute you. You and your comrades will always be remembered.

Stephen Cooper
Merville Barracks, August 2020

"Reg Curtis was a Grenadier Guardsman, and his loyalty to his Regiment and to its standards and traditions never wavered, though he spent most of his war service with the Parachute Regiment. I was his Commanding Officer in North Africa and Sicily, and he was amongst the few who survived from the 1st Para Battalion in what was probably the hardest fighting in the last war, in the mountains and cork forests of Tunisia. Reg Curtis will always be remembered by those of us who were fortunate to know him and serve with him, and I for one had this inestimable privilege."

Brigadier Alastair Pearson CB DSO*** OBE MC KStJ TD
CO 1st Parachute Battalion 1942-43
CO 8th Parachute Battalion 1944

"Reg Curtis was one of the first among many of a gallant band of brothers in arms who were happy to serve their King and Country. They established and maintained the high tradition of the Parachute Regiment and Airborne forces throughout the last world war. There are many others like Reg Curtis in the two great regiments in which he has been so proud to serve. May they all be greatly blessed for their courage and fortitude."

Brigadier James Ledger Hill DSO** MC
CO 1st Parachute Battalion 1942
Commander 3rd Parachute Brigade 1943-45

"In attack most daring, in defence most cunning, in endurance most steadfast, they performed a feat of arms which will be remembered and recounted as long as the virtues of courage and resolution have power to move the hearts of men."

Sir Winston Churchill

Author's Preface

This is a story told through one man's eyes. There are so many different memories held by others, but these are mine. In my 94th year they remain vivid and clear, often more so than recollections of more recent times. I suppose that's the way it is when you have lived through war. This is a story that begins before the Second World War and runs through it—a time when everyone did their bit and I just played my part.

I was already in the Grenadier Guards when war was declared with Germany in September 1939, and when Winston Churchill's call to volunteer for commando and parachute training came in 1940 it was an easy one to answer. I was privileged to serve my country and am proud to have done so with other pioneers of the Parachute Regiment, whose memory and friendship I hold dear. I have no regrets.

Between 1939 and 1945 we took part in the greatest conflict in human history. We won the war, of course, and back home in Britain have now had almost 70 years of peace, for which we can all be grateful. What a shame it is, though, that even the vast scale of suffering we went through was not enough to finally put an end to war itself. I don't suppose there will ever be one way of agreeing about everything but I can't help hoping that things will eventually get better for everyone, not just us.

This is a book made possible by events but more especially by people. I have been blessed over the years to be surrounded by good people and I thank and acknowledge them all. First, my family, and above all my wife Betty Frances, who has been a complete part of my life and without doubt my rock. I hope my numerous other family members will forgive my not listing every name, but you are all embedded in my heart. To those who have contributed, whether directly or indirectly, to the making of this book, I offer unqualified thanks for your patience and encouragement.

After my service with the Guards I was one of the first recruits for No. 2 Commando, which later became the 11th SAS, then the 1st Parachute Battalion, then part of the 1st Parachute Brigade, which in turn formed part of the Parachute Regiment. I trained and fought with many good men, a lot of them becoming close friends, and including far too many who did not survive the war as I did. I thank every one of you for giving me the precious gift of another seventy years of life.

I took part in the Parachute Regiment's most remembered battle at Arnhem in September 1944 and share deeply in our bond with the good people of that city. This is an unbreakable bond that grows ever stronger and now truly spans generations. I must have returned to Arnhem 30 times since 1944 and I doubt there is any place on earth where friendship is more profound. I'm sure I can speak for every Para when I say thank you to the citizens of Arnhem, especially to the wonderful children. There is no sight more moving than your annual laying of flowers at the Airborne Cemetery. You are our bridge to the future.

When the war ended I found it difficult initially knuckling down to civilian life. The letter from the government saying, 'you are now a civilian' seemed so sudden. I couldn't face the prospect of an office job, so tried manufacturing—making handbags—before joining my brother-in-law John in his landscape gardening business, and then branching out on my own in the same line of work. Having an artificial leg didn't help but I didn't let it hinder me, and the limb-fitting centre at Gillingham kindly reinforced my artificial knee for kneeling, several times! I got a BSA motorbike and sidecar and had the gears modified to operate by hand instead of foot. I built my own house. You do the best you can. Many people have helped me along the way and continue to do so. To each of you, thank you for your every kindness and for your friendship. I hope you will enjoy reading this book.

Reg Curtis

Chapter One
Prelude to War

My arrival into the world on September the 11th, 1920 took place at 113 Rushey Green, Catford, South East London, only a stone's throw from the old Lewisham Hippodrome, where I would later spend many an enjoyable evening. I lost my mother when I was three years old, so my father, for a while, had a bit of a time going from pillar to post. Then he married again, and in 1930 we moved to a semi-detached house at Grove Park, quite near to the hospital. The three-bedroomed semi was mortgaged for £400. My father worked as a clerk at a wholesale distributor of electrical components and light fittings. His weekly wage of just under four pounds does not sound much today, but he paid the mortgage, ran a Triumph motorbike with sidecar, we went to the cinema once a week, and we all ate very well.

As a youth, I carried out a milk round in the early morning and a newspaper round in the evening, earning four shillings a week, which helped towards the cost of the special clothing I needed as a choirboy at Saint Augustine's Church near Grove Park railway station. When I left school in 1934 at the age of fourteen I got a job at Elliot Brothers, an electrical and mechanical engineers in Lewisham. I cycled the five miles to and from work, Monday to Saturday, and learnt quickly under the watchful eye of the charge hand, learning how to operate a milling machine, centre lathe and hydraulic press, and finally working as a capstan setter operator.

After three years, I was beginning to settle in for a long-term job with good remuneration when a series of small strikes put the damper on my enthusiasm. The persistent industrial action prompted my decision to join the Army, where such strikes were not tolerated. My father had been in the Royal Army Service Corps and my grandfather was chairman of the local Royal British Legion, so the Army seemed natural enough in my family. I was encouraged by my Uncle Fred, himself a regimental sergeant major. I chose the Foot Guards because after a short term of service I would be acceptable to the City of London Police. In those days you also had to be at least 5' 10½" to be a policeman. I was already 6' 1", and still growing. I presented myself to the Guards Recruiting Office in London and enlisted with the First, or Grenadier, Regiment of Foot Guards.

My first stop was the Guards Depot in Caterham, Surrey, where I immediately had to get used to the bellowing of orders and everything being carried out in double-quick time. For 18 weeks we went through endless seemingly unnecessary military manoeuvres at the screaming command of an NCO and I didn't know if I was coming or going for a while. There was one Corporal Tucker, my squad instructor, who took great delight in marching us on to the frozen parade ground with extra zest, then put us on a charge if we slipped up—so you not only received a sore rump but got extra parade as punishment. Another approach was to march us towards a large puddle and then give the order to 'mark time'. 'Come on! Knees higher!' he would shout from a safe distance, scrutinizing each man in turn and looking for any signs of cracking. We were just numbers at Caterham, though to this day I say it did me no harm, as it instilled a self-discipline that has served me well through life.

After my Depot training, I was posted to Victoria Barracks, Windsor, where discipline was still tough but the pace, thank goodness, slowed down. I carried out guard duty at Windsor Castle and various fatigues, some of which were more leisurely and pleasant than others. These included private garden party duty, during which, clad in the finery of the Guards red tunic and bearskin, I was required to diplomatically step between any royalty and would-be photographer, politely asking that no photographs be taken. Royal family baggage fatigue was another interesting one. I recall unloading the royal baggage from a lorry outside Windsor Castle and taking down a round box marked 'Queen Mary's Boot Box' and a bicycle labelled 'HRH Princess Elizabeth', which I sat on and rode for a few yards, just for devilment. On this fatigue we had to wear black Army-issue plimsolls inside the castle, except in the royal apartments, where even these were to be removed. By tradition, the handlers of the royal baggage received one brand new shilling and a good meal, so after work we sat down with the castle staff and were served a meal fit for a king!

While at Windsor in 1938 I had the pleasure to appear in a film about the reign of Queen Victoria, entitled *Sixty Glorious Years*. Some of the scenes were set at or around the entrance to the Castle from Windsor Great Park and the approach to the East Terrace. We used our second-best tunics, bearskin caps, Lee Enfield rifles, and, to suit the period, were loaned white trousers by the film company. Anna Neagle was the star of the film, playing Queen Victoria, and I was included in shots where a sentry was required. I began to like the life of a film star, or at least that of an 'extra', which was quite a contrast to being a machine operator in Lewisham, or for that matter to becoming a real soldier.

Soon enough, I left the glamour of Windsor and the comfort of Victoria Barracks behind and was sent to Pirbright in Surrey, where every Guardsman goes for fieldcraft work and firing on the open range. It was my duty to be able to handle and fire a gun in preparation to protect King and Country in an emergency, but trust my luck to have fallen foul of bad weather. It was not really my cup of tea to prostrate myself on a wet and windswept firing range with a sergeant breathing down my neck whispering words of encouragement, and the added supply of rainwater running over me in torrents from his groundsheet cape. It must have done some good as I made a first class shot, though for what purpose I was not yet sure. Thankfully, in my spare time I was able to get away to Woking, Guildford and Farnborough, all within five miles reach. I made friends with another Guardsman by the name of Collet and we enjoyed making the rounds of the local pubs, cafés, dance halls and cinemas, and went on an altogether different kind of manoeuvre in the pleasant parks with the occasional girls we met.

I returned to Windsor for a short spell before moving with the rest of my Battalion to Wellington and Chelsea Barracks in London and a tour of public duty. This included guard duty at Buckingham Palace, St. James' Palace, the Bank of England and the Tower of London. Of them all, I think I preferred Buckingham Palace, which seemed such a grand, majestic place. On the occasion of the visit to London of the King of the Belgians I was chosen to take part in the Guard of Honour. King's Rules and Regulations stated that one was required to look straight ahead when being inspected, but I found myself looking the King straight in the eyes when he confronted me. I think I wanted to be sure of a close look at a foreign sovereign.

In 1938 I participated in one ceremonial parade that is a must for every Guardsman—the monarch's birthday parade, or 'Trooping the Colour'. Dating back to the 17th Century, this takes place in London each year in June. We trained for it in earnest and, except for the usual guard duties and fatigues, worked at it continuously until we knew the drill backwards. When the day came, it was an extraordinary personal experience to march up the Mall from Horse Guards Parade towards Buckingham Palace with King George VI riding at our head. I think my chest must have gained at least another four inches.

I now realised the importance of all that 'bull' we had to put up with at Caterham—all that running around at the double in ever increasing circles and the obsession with fastidious appearance and instant obedience. 'Once a Guardsman, always a Guardsman', Drill Sergeant Cook had bellowed in my ear whilst prancing around me like a proud peacock on the barrack square, glaring and looking me up and down for any defects, his horrible face so close that I could almost count the number of hairs on his thick bristle moustache. I certainly felt like a Guardsman now, and was immensely proud of it.

Later that year the Czechoslovakian crisis presented the unexpected prospect of travel to a foreign country and we were put on standby to go out there on policing duty. We were even issued with the necessary uniforms and equipment, but in the event did not go. I did, however, enjoy some foreign hospitality in a group of 30 serving British Grenadiers invited to be guests of the

Belgian Grenadiers. We had a great time in Brussels, where we were lavishly wined and dined and, for good measure, each provided with a mademoiselle to show us the city at night. I remember my first taste of frogs' legs soup.

Early in 1939 I was transferred to the home of the British Army at Aldershot in Hampshire, where I settled into some more 'square-bashing' on its vast parade ground. It was here that we practised for the Aldershot Tattoo, which was to take place in June. We were put through our paces for hours on end by Regimental Sergeant Major Swan. I felt quite diminutive in the middle of that parade ground, despite being among the tallest men in the Brigade of Guards. I'll never forget the atmosphere on the night of the Tattoo when our Battalion marched on, dressed in navy blue trousers with red piping down the outside seam of each trouser leg, long sleeved white waiter-type jackets with brass buttons, and the Guards peaked cap with red band around the crown. Carried out without a word of command, our drill display lasted for twenty minutes, the finale being the only time a command was given: 'The Battalion will advance in review order—by the centre—quick march!' Four hundred and fifty men moved as one.

In August some mysterious goings-on began. Unusual apparatus in the form of digging equipment—both powered and hand-operated—appeared, along with wheelbarrows and mountains of little sacks, which turned out to be sandbags. Lorries loaded with sand would dump their contents at various points and, instead of the usual drill parades and kit inspections, we found ourselves filling these bags with sand and building barriers. I thought it must be some sort of giant exercise and had no idea that it was in preparation for a real enemy. Being confined to the barracks area, with its own shops and theatre, we didn't mix with the public, so knew very little about matters of national importance. Indeed, in those days a serviceman was not allowed to discuss politics and would be put on a charge if caught attending a political meeting.

On the 3rd of September, war was declared with Germany and I realised what all the sandbagging was for. Within days my Battalion was mobilised, reservists were called up, and, along with thousands of other troops, two weeks later we were in France. The visit would prove to be exciting but costly. It would last in my case for 254 days and end with evacuation from Dunkirk the following May. I think I was quite unperturbed at the possibility of getting killed—after all, I was a soldier, trained to kill, so why should I have any qualms?

Chapter Two
With the British Expeditionary Force

My 3rd Battalion Grenadier Guards, under Major Allan Adair, was in the 1st Guards Brigade commanded by Brigadier Merton Beckwith-Smith, being part of the 1st Division of the British Expeditionary Force. As we disembarked at Cherbourg on a cold and wet September day, my recollection is of a great concourse of shipping of varying shapes and tonnage heaving at the quayside and a conglomeration of men and vehicles shunting to and fro before disappearing up side turnings, destination unknown. The younger men like me were a little wide-eyed and looked with eager interest at their new surroundings. The older men knew what it was all about and did not welcome being torn from family life in England and thrust into yet another conflict.

Heavily laden in 'field service marching order', which comprised all the gear needed for the battlefront, we clambered into lorries and soon left the port. It was getting dark, so I could not take in the scenery very well. After a long and uncomfortable journey of about 500 kilometres, stopping at given points for food and exercise, we arrived near the Belgian border, close to the city of Lille. Here we stayed, carrying out ammunition and border guard duty, along with other tasks, including building and disguising fortifications. We even constructed a house, complete with glass windows, around a massive pillbox. For non-tradesmen, we made a pretty good job of it.

Activity along the border increased with the infiltration of fifth columnists and spies, and our daily orders were to be constantly on the lookout for Germans posing as British officers or farm workers. I challenged and arrested one such officer who omitted to remember to put pips on his epaulette before wandering around our positions. He spoke in faultless English, but that lack of pips bothered me and I asked him to accompany me to the guardroom. I later heard that this so-called captain was unable to satisfy our gentlemen of the Military Intelligence.

Before long, we were moved up to Metz, only about 50 miles from the border with Luxembourg, and a similar distance from the German town of Merzig in the Saarbrucken. The surroundings were totally different to Lille. When we arrived the weather was appalling, with a thick blanket of snow everywhere. Most of the population had moved out and the place looked desolate. Using an old warehouse as our headquarters and guardroom, with outbuildings as temporary sleeping quarters, we endured freezing conditions. All taps and pipes were frozen through lack of heating or maintenance. I had to break the ice in a horse trough to get shaving water.

I was selected to be in a 20-strong fighting patrol, which was to operate in the area of the Maginot and Siegfried Lines—the respective French and German fortifications. It was here, when we were preparing to move to the forward positions of the Maginot Line, that I noticed a French Citroen car some 50 yards along the road and a smart-looking woman in her thirties, chatting to groups of French and English soldiers. She looked quite something in her long fur coat. 'What a doll', I thought. But such thoughts were interrupted by a rather hysterical young lieutenant screaming, 'Stop! Stop that woman! Stop her!' The woman turned hesitantly and then quickened her step towards me and a Guardsman named Elms. As she fumbled in her black envelope-type handbag, we grabbed an arm each and I snatched the bag from her. She did not protest very much, just: 'You silly boys, what are you doing?' I was beginning to enjoy the aroma of her perfume when the lieutenant lumbered up panting, with a sergeant close at his heels, and promptly took her into custody. Such a beautiful spy!

In the forward positions we took over a deserted village called Tromborn, about six miles from the German border. The inhabitants had clearly made a very hasty departure. In some cases, tables were untouched, the remains of a meal still on them. Beds were unmade, as if their owners had only just tumbled out, and wardrobes swung open with a few garments left hanging on pegs. We were allowed to take food or anything else of use to the war effort. As it was snowing, our fighting patrol decided to make use of sheets to create sets of camouflage gear: white suits, gloves, over-boots, hats and coverings for our rifles. Hunting around, I found a sewing machine, thinking that we may as well do things the easy way. When everyone had finished using this, I returned it with a note: 'Thanks for the use of your machine. I return it, but it does not do a very good seam!' The white gear was quite natty and we pranced around, rather fancying ourselves as 'Alpine' troops. Anyway, it did the job and made us less conspicuous in the snow.

As a fighting patrol we didn't fire a shot; it was more a matter of listening and night reconnaissance. In our white outfits, carrying only rifles and limited other gear, we travelled more comfortably than we had previously. On one night reconnaissance we became overconfident and one of our lads knocked up against the enemy wire. It was a still, bright, moonlit night. We were in no-man's land, just 75 feet from the forward German positions. Their talking stopped abruptly. As luck would have it, we were crawling, so we froze, hugging the ground for an hour without moving. I was frantic during most of that time because of a tickle developing in my throat. I kept cramming snow in my mouth to ease it, and must have sucked through a couple of cubic feet of the stuff, avoiding coughing only with considerable difficulty. When we heard whispered words of German command, our patrol leader gave the silent signal to move on, which we did with some relief.

On another occasion, we were on our way back to base, when, from the direction of a bend in the road fifty yards away, we saw a group of figures. We were about two miles from our lines and knew that no other patrols were out, so these men must be the enemy. Our patrol leader gave the signal to lie still. We were straddled each side of the road in semi-open ground, but fortunately the night was not too bright. The group passed by, ten men in all, spaced six to eight feet apart. They were well armed but wore no white suits. Keeping them in view and moving only our eyes, we lay unnoticed. If we had been spotted they would have had the advantage because of their automatic weapons, and also the fact that as they passed down our centre we could not have fired on them for fear of hitting our own men.

Spending Christmas 1939 in the outposts of the Maginot Line was not everyone's idea of a pleasant Noël. In the New Year, my unit moved back to the Belgian border area, not far from a French town called Douai, where guarding ammunition dumps and border checkpoints were our main tasks. In March, I was glad of ten days' home leave, but it was only a brief respite and I was soon back in France.

Over the border, lights were still blazing in Belgian towns, while on our side we had a strictly enforced blackout. I was on border checkpoint early in April when a Belgian woman of about 50 years of age waddled along, a shawl hugging her head and shoulders. I greeted her with a 'Bonjour Madame', but she just glared at me and spat at my feet, shouting about 'English' something or other. She started to gesticulate with raised arm and open palm in the direction of Belgium and screamed at me: 'La Boche ici! La Boche ici tout de suite!' Then she spat once more and went on her way. Charming soul, I thought.

German parachutists landed at Nivelles in Belgium on the 10th of May, preceded by prolonged bombing, an action which prompted our subsequent move into Belgium. A small rear echelon party was left to tidy up and bring forward necessary supplies as and when required, while our Guards Battalion, along with the remainder of the Division, pushed on through Belgium to Louvain, some 60 miles from the German border. The going was pretty easy until we arrived in the Louvain area. Here things began to turn against us, with aerial bombings, shellfire and occasional machine gun fire. The whole area seemed to be dotted with Germans—units of motorised infantry and Panzers of the German 6th Army. They were just 600 yards off, and after a while one of our companies made physical contact with them. Over the next couple of days, we strategically withdrew out of the town.

When I came into contact with two Germans for the first time myself, I gave them five rounds of rapid fire at a range of fifty yards as they edged towards me under cover of garden walls and fencing. They were my first shots in anger. I didn't see the two Germans any more, so maybe they were lucky shots. Guardsmen Bateman and Elms doubled past and shouted for me to come on and we continued into open country, making our way over a bridge and halting after roughly 1,000 yards, where we took up defensive positions.

Air activity was increasing tremendously. Messerschmitt 109s were machine-gunning at low level and had strafed our troops coming over the bridge only a few minutes after I crossed. Then, four Stuka dive-bombers, either bad at bomb aiming or not wishing to hit the bridge, dropped their bombs on each side of the approach road. Unbeknown to us, sappers of the Royal Engineers had attached explosives to the bridge and word went around that it would be blown in 15 minutes. Corporal Gooch of the Grenadier Guards slid by, telling us to keep our heads down. 'At a thousand yards we should be safe as houses', I joked with Sergeant Wood. 'All the same, keep your head down, son', he wisely told me. Then there was a terrific explosion and you could no longer see the bridge for dust and smoke. A few seconds later I heard a weird whirring sound getting quickly nearer—then, with a thud here and a *phlut* there, lumps of masonry as big as footballs were dropping around me. One lump, a foot square, landed just 30 feet away. When the smoke cleared, the bridge had been blown in two places.

Leaving the area and travelling mainly on foot, encountering few enemy on the ground but experiencing continuous shelling and bombing from the air, we came to a stop by the River Escaut, near the city of Tournai, six miles from the French border. Here, we went into a counterattack, during which a very well liked platoon commander, Lieutenant the Duke of Northumberland, was killed.

Lance Corporal Harry Nicholls and Guardsman Nash were ordered to flush out some bothersome machine gun nests 600 yards from our positions. The section I was in gave covering fire. To our left, they picked their way with caution, Nicholls with a light machine gun under each arm. I didn't see them anymore but they must have completed the mission because the enemy fire ceased after a while. Lance Corporal Nicholls was posted missing, presumed killed, but later reported as being alive in enemy hands. He was awarded the Victoria Cross for this action. In the semi-built-up area on the river, the Germans afforded very good target practice for me. I found that I just could not miss. But we were all getting weary through lack of sleep and proper food—no one can live off scraps or from scavenging for long without feeling the worse for it—and enemy numbers were increasing tenfold, or so it seemed.

Continuing on, we came to another stop at or near the Ypres-Comines Line. This would be the last time I took part in a coordinated attack with the 3rd Battalion Grenadier Guards. We went into a bayonet charge at Kortekeer. Setting off, I felt very scared and all sorts of things went through my mind, like 'what the hell am I doing here? Oh yes, I joined the Army to become a policeman—what a laugh!' The muck was flying fast, bullets whining and splattering, and I crouched lower to dodge them. On I went with the rest, my 16-inch Lee

Enfield bayonet blade fixed and protruding at the ready. Ready! Ready for what? The only thing I had ever stuck with a bayonet was a sack dummy. Then I saw them in the swirling smoke: human beings, not sacks—real Germans. Blimey! I trudged on, wrenching my ankle in a pothole, on and on until the order rang out: 'Charge! Charge!' I began to double now with my bayonet thrust at full 'on guard', those figures growing bigger and bigger until they were just a few yards away amid the din and yells of pain. There were dead bodies from both sides littering my approach. I was a foot from two Germans when, suddenly, they both dropped their rifles and reached very high, chattering something about 'comrade'. I was so bloody amazed and relieved that I said, 'Come on then, I'll take you prisoner!'

My Battalion was now badly cut up, with numbers well below effective fighting power, and we were ordered to attach ourselves to any unit and make our way to Dunkirk, though no reason was given. And here was I stuck with two German prisoners. The journey was nerve-racking, with hordes of refugees jamming the roads and making military transport movement almost impossible. Lorries, guns and French H.39 Hotchkiss tanks were often seen abandoned in ditches, rendered immobile but clearly not by enemy action. What was going on? Were we throwing in the towel?

Two other infantrymen, Mick and George, became attached to me to help out with the prisoners, and when night was upon us I managed to get a couple of hours' sleep. Being the oldest soldier I assumed command, which the others accepted readily. Together with the two Germans, we made ourselves useful by giving a hand to tip British lorries, tanks and artillery guns into a canal running alongside the road—anything to prevent the equipment being collected with ease and used again by the enemy. The route was an absolute shambles, with military and civilian gear constantly getting entangled.

Passing through a small town called Wormhoudt, 20 miles from Dunkirk, the aftermath of bombing was evident. Civilians and military alike looked weary and decidedly non-composed. A group of French soldiers spotted our captives and started to approach menacingly. Sensing an awkward predicament, I ushered the two Germans into a doorway and gave my two infantry lads the order: 'On-guard, and keep this lot at bay!' I stood in the centre with my rifle trailed. The Germans behind me shuffled their feet uneasily. How ridiculous it seemed to be protecting the enemy, but they were in my charge and it was not for me to decide their fate. The French soldiers halted at my raised hand. 'Bonjour', I said with assured confidence. 'Cigarette, Messieurs?' I offered a packet; they took the lot. I was a good four inches taller than any of the Frenchmen, and the psychological trick appeared to do the work of calming them. Looking me up and down, they went on their way, still ranting about 'Les Boches' and leaving in their wake a strong smell of French wine.

Rumours were plentiful now, such as the story that Leopold III of Belgium and his army were capitulating. Towns all over France were falling into enemy hands. French General Giraud had been taken prisoner. To pile on the agony, the Germans did not let up on their bombing or machine-gunning one bit, and their slaughter of refugees was unnecessary and sickening to see. We did what we could in the way of tending civilian wounded, using their own clothing or bedding for bandages, while the dead were either left or covered with something to hide their torn bodies and agonised faces. Even cattle grazing in the fields had not escaped the blitzkrieg and lay bloated through lack of milking, or blown apart by shellfire. The carnage spread for a good two miles. After seeing those poor wretched civilians so cut up, the occasional wounded soldier did not seem quite so bad. My two German prisoners appeared to be as disgusted by all of this as I was.

We reached the outskirts of Dunkirk to find a mass build-up of French and British soldiers, with transport, tanks and artillery pieces jamming the roads like a London rush hour. Trudging on, still with my two prisoners, I could not help but look twice and smile at the familiar name of a café, which for a moment provided a pleasant memory of Manchester: the *Café Belle Vue*. But the next five days were a mixture of hell, hunger and fatigue and I think it was only thanks to the fatigue that I overcame the hell and hunger. I know it was five days because I put a nick in my rifle butt each morning when roused by the visiting Stukas and Messerschmitts.

During daylight, the appointed Beach Master, a British officer, mustered officers and NCOs from all regiments and briefed them to organise parties of men to tend the wounded, bury the dead, and scavenge for ammunition and food. I found it most distasteful removing tins of bully beef and biscuit remains from corpses, but at least I still had my life. The beach was littered with abandoned lorries and trucks, as well as Army staff-cars with wheels missing and doors hanging off. As I wandered around, going about my task among those mutilated forms that once were carefree young men, I remember thinking that I must be dreaming.

I was brought back sharply to reality by the appearance of two enemy fighter planes, which proceeded to distribute even more death and panic. I dived over a corpse and slithered down a sand dune—the staring eyes of the corpse seeming to say, 'get your head down and arse up!' Out of the corner of my eye I noticed, protruding out of the sand, a Hotchkiss 1914 machine gun, as used by the French forces. I buried myself in the sand, not that this would have done me much good, as bullets just zipped through and sought out anyone whose number was up. Apparently, this time mine was not.

After five days on the beaches, it was a relief to find that it was finally my turn to get into the snake-like line of troops readying for departure. The evacuation had been going on steadily, despite the fact that numerous ships had been lost to enemy fire. Upon our arrival at Dunkirk, Mick and George had gone off to try and locate their own regiments, while my two German prisoners were boarded on a ship before me. Maybe this was to their advantage, but maybe not because I saw a number of vessels hit by enemy bombing and machine-gunning. One such stricken ship received a Stuka bomb directly down the funnel. It must have been a good thousand yards out, but I could see small human dots falling over the side. In all, some 40 various ships were sunk or damaged at Dunkirk.

It was about 10.30 on the morning of the 30th of May that I found myself shuffling along the sand with almost as much sand in my boots as there was outside. I slipped and slopped about and could feel a couple of holes in my socks. I was now very near the spot where soldiers were entering the water for that long-awaited last journey to relative safety aboard a ship, and home. On reaching the point of entry, I saw two ropes anchored into the sand and stretching 200 yards out to a ship. They sagged in the centre to occasionally disappear in the lapping murky water, helmets registering the presence of soldiers along the rope line. While I eagerly, though uneasily, waited to enter the water and join that line, I noticed nearby an ingenious improvised pier constructed of abandoned transport, with builders' planks and lorry tailboards attached for walking over. But German bombers had put a stop to that, as it was badly holed and no longer in use.

'Right, soldier!' The sharp but almost gentle order rang in my ears. 'In you go, keep moving.' I started off into that cold uninviting water, slinging my rifle over my head so that it was carried on my back, and enabling me to have both hands free to grasp the rope. I was about halfway now and the water felt very cold, my weary body heavy with the wet clothing. Clinging on for dear life, the water squelched in my boots, which, although cold, gave some relief after wearing them day and night for the past two weeks.

As I drew closer to the vast mass of a ship—a minesweeper—heaving in the mucky-looking swell I could see its multi-barrel ack-ack gun pointing skyward in readiness for any Stuka or fighter attack, the operators seemingly oblivious to our presence. One was scanning the sky with his binoculars. The water by now was well and truly up to my neck and I still had 50 feet to go. I clung to the rope with both hands and pushed on. The man behind gave me a shove. The water kept lapping over my nose, into my eyes. Gulping, choking and spitting out endless mouthfuls of oily, foul-tasting salt water, I was now quite submerged. With a last mighty effort I lunged in the direction of the boat, still grasping that rope. It could not have been more than a minute that I was under the water but it felt like a lifetime. Clinging on tight to the rope with my left hand, with my right I groped for the rope mesh hanging down the side of the ship, and with great exultation found and grabbed it.

I managed to pull myself up—up—and up, the ship rocking and heaving with each vibration of the exploding bombs, which were arriving much too close for my liking. Then, eager hands reached out and I was in the grasp of two burly bearded seamen. I went limp and fell in a heap on the deck, silently thanking God that I had made it. 'Come on mate', a seaman called from a few feet away. 'Make way for the rest. Move along, please. There's more room up forward.' As I moved along, I looked in the direction of Calais and wondered how things were going for my brother-in-law Tony, who was there with the Queen Victoria Rifles.

Flopping down exhausted, I was soon asleep, though, inevitably, we had a visit from a Messerschmitt, and this woke me violently as its bullets danced along the ship's deck, causing large pieces of wood splinters to spew over everyone. These administered as much damage as the bullets to some unfortunate recipients. The replying firepower from the surrounding ships, including the pom-pom on our own ship, which burst into action just above my head, was most reassuring. I dozed off again and slept like a log until we docked in England, unaware of the fact that the guns had opened up on three further occasions while I slept.

So ended my participation with more than 300,000 others in 'Operation Dynamo', better known to history as 'the miracle of Dunkirk'.

Chapter Three
A New Type of Fighting Soldier

There followed two weeks of leave that I enjoyed more than ever before (the sheer ecstasy of white sheets and pint after pint of beautiful beer!) and the days of roughing it in France soon seemed so very long ago. Then I returned to duty, reporting to Louth, near Grimsby, where I met up with my now reinforced Battalion, which could not have included many more than 50 familiar faces. The rest were young new blood and had not yet seen an angry German. Made up to unpaid lance corporal, I carried out anti-paratroop patrol, performed guard duty at vital points and went on a section leaders' course—all a cakewalk after past experiences.

In August I received a telegram telling me that my home in South London had been hit by a sea mine and I was given compassionate leave to return. What the hell was a sea mine doing inland? It must be a mistake, I thought. However, apparently there was such a thing, which came down attached to a parachute. It was dark when I arrived at London's King's Cross to find that no public transport was running and an air raid was in progress. After a few enquiries and listening to as many bright suggestions, I decided to start walking home—it was only ten miles, which seemed nothing after all the miles slogged in France.

Bombers were droning overhead when I reached Westminster Bridge. They sounded like Dorniers to me, giving off their rattling throb caused by unsynchronized engines. Searchlights were fanning the sky trying to seek them out and ack-ack guns were barking, with occasional lumps of shrapnel from their bursting shells playing across the rooftops and pranging against wall and pavement. I started running across the bridge, not so much because I was frightened but because, as at Dunkirk, I couldn't swim. After a hike to Lewisham, I took a breather in a pub that was being used as an ARP (air raid precautions) centre, where I downed a pint of beer, paid for by a kindly policeman. It went down very well at two in the morning. Then at Lee Green I called in at the local police station to use the washroom facilities. After a cup of tea with the duty sergeant, I was talked into staying put for a short while in one of the cells. 'You may as well', he said. 'You'll get to Grove Park too early to knock anyone up'. It was around six when he roused me with another cup of tea, just before the all clear sounded. This was great—a policeman waiting on me, and a sergeant at that. He didn't make bad tea either.

Upon reaching Grove Park, as I turned into Fairfield Road I saw immediately that our house had received a direct hit. There was now just a heap of debris where once had stood half a dozen houses, and dozens more were badly damaged. The local ARP warden told me that not one person had been killed because everyone had taken to their Anderson air raid shelters; my parents were both OK and staying with some friends a mile up the road. It was a shock to see our home destroyed, but after all I had seen in France I think I must have become immune to any real emotions. I stayed for a few days, to see my parents and salvage what possessions I could from the ruins. I managed to find a few things: a wrist watch still going beneath two feet of rubble, my school football boots, an electric light bulb in working order. Not much. Then I returned to Louth.

In October, as a result of a directive sent out by Prime Minister Winston Churchill, we received a letter, which was read out to us by the regimental sergeant major. 'Volunteers', he shouted, 'for a new type of fighting soldier are required'. He glanced over the top of the paper, beady eyes registering some amusement. 'Soldiers', he carried on, 'to be trained as commandos and parachutists. Now I know that you would not wish to desert the Regiment, but anyone wishing to volunteer, one pace forward, march!' Glaring as he did so, he took three stealthy steps towards us. 'Well? You all chicken, then?' There was not a titter, nor even a hesitant shuffle. I thought back to the days in France. I thought of the carnage, of Calais, of the British prisoners of war of the Warwick Regiment herded into a field just outside Dunkirk and machine-gunned to death by the Waffen SS. I thought of my home being blown to smithereens, and how the Germans were blocking my ambition to become a London policeman. I took a pace forward before it was too late.

Weeks went by without any notification of a move on the new venture. Christmas came and the Battalion sat down to an excellent dinner with all the trimmings in the village hall. Then, a few days later, along with two others, I was called to the C.O.'s office and told that I would shortly be on my way. Where to, I would know on the day of departure. He gave us a pep talk about never forgetting we were Guardsmen, and upholding the Regiment's traditions at all times. At first he seemed to challenge us to dare thinking of leaving, then his expression and tone changed as he welcomed our acceptance of the wonderful opportunity. I could read his thoughts. Why not go out and carry on spreading the deeds of the Regiment to others in this new adventure? He wished us luck, saying that maybe we would meet in action some day.

It was in July 1940 at the height of the Battle of Britain that the Prime Minister had issued the directive ordering this new type of fighting soldier—units to be trained as parachute troops, whose main role would be to spearhead the eventual re-conquest of Europe. The War Office adopted the Commando system to give effect to the directive and I was to join No. 2 Commando, later renamed the 11th Special Air Service Battalion, and still later the 1st Parachute Battalion.

An organisation called the Central Landing Establishment was formed, comprising both British Army and Royal Air Force units—the Army being responsible for ground training and the RAF for parachuting. In Britain at that time there was little or no knowledge of the techniques of parachuting, so everything had to be thought out very carefully. There were no special types of parachutes for jumping from aircraft, and no suitable aircraft. The whole lot had to be devised, developed and tested, all too often with fatal casualties or severe injuries. Eventually the success of the undertaking would make it possible for the Commander-in-Chief to have two fully-trained Airborne divisions at his disposal on 'D' Day—the 1st and the 6th. It has been said that the interdependence and cooperation between the British Army and the RAF in the production of these divisions in so short a space of time, and having started from scratch, is an inter-Service achievement unmatched before or since.

In early January 1941, I was on my way to Ringway, near Manchester, which was to be our centre of training.

I first spent a short while in Congleton, where I met up with more volunteers from Guards units and other regiments. There, we were formed into what was to be called 'L' Troop of No. 2 Commando, under the command of a Guards officer, Captain Bromley-Martin. We were equipped with new gear and carried out a few exercises involving the Home Guard, but our stay was brief and we soon set off for Ringway, pleased that we were getting a stage nearer to becoming para-commandos.

At Ringway, after reporting in at the hangar, we were fixed up with civilian accommodation in nearby Wythenshawe. The other volunteers included quite a few Guardsmen from the Welsh, Coldstream and Irish Regiments, and all had seen active service. There was some 'leg-pulling' between Guards and other regiments, and each had its own traditions to live up to and defended those loyalties with vigour. Very soon, though, a new relationship began to mould and an *esprit de corps* developed which was quite different to that of our parent regiments.

Later that month, our Commanding Officer, Lieutenant-Colonel C.I.A. Jackson, sent us packing to Scotland—to Fort William in Inverness—to carry out a special commando endurance test. We were to spend four weeks at an isolated place named Achnacarry. As we waited at Fort William for transport to take us on to this camp, it was raining cats and dogs and we were hungry. After a seemingly long time, three trucks wheeled to a stop in front of us, and in so doing went through a large puddle and drenched a couple of lads. 'You twot', said one, 'What the hell do you...' He cut the remark short when he noticed three stripes on the arm of the driver, who had jumped down and was now confronting him with, 'You were saying, son?' This bloke's a right so-and-so, I thought to myself. He sported a Royal Artillery cap badge. 'Sorry, Sarge, I didn't see…' said the wet lad, but before he could say more the sergeant bellowed, 'Right, you lousy lot, into the trucks at the double. If anyone is left with his feet on the ground by the time I have finished counting to five, you can walk to the camp!' By the time he had got to four, everyone was on board and the sergeant had slammed the tailboard shut, shouting with a grin, 'Hold tight, it's a rough ride!'

I am sure it was a planned rough ride. We spent something like ninety minutes going round in circles, swaying violently from one side of the road to the other, hitting mounds and sinking into potholes. Presumably, it was all part of the test. Turning off the road, the ride now became much smoother until at last we slid ten feet to a stop. The sergeant appeared at the back of the truck and shouted for us to dismount. Our nice, clean boots were about to be baptised in four inches of mud. On jumping down, I saw that the sergeant himself had changed into wellingtons.

So this was Achnacarry. What a dump! There were a dozen or so wooden huts—uninviting places, with wisps of dirty smoke billowing out of mean-looking chimney pots. By the look of it, they were burning old rope, and quite possibly they were. Part of our training was to fend for ourselves, and that included finding our own kindling. Now we settled down to some real soldiering and I actually began to enjoy the tests thrust upon us. I didn't realise at first that we were being used as human guinea pigs, trying out new methods of roughing it and of delivering a soldier to the place of battle. For everyone it was a test of strength, involving guts, sheer cunning and a determination to win through. Some conditions were abominable but my conscience told me this was a challenge I must rise to.

Two whole weeks were spent out in the wilds of the Scottish Highlands on the rough and mountainous slopes around Ben Nevis, the highest mountain in the British Isles and a place for the very hardy only. The area is barren at any time of the year, but this was January. The main area of our training took in Loch Laggan, Loch Lochy, the River Spey, Glen Roy and Aberchalder, a 20-mile-sided triangle with Spean Bridge at the western point, Laggan at the eastern and Fort Augustus at the northern.

Our minimum rations of condensed foods in small cubes could produce quite a tasty mess tin of soup or porridge when heated in water. The special stove we had was very small too, just four inches in diameter by three inches high, and was one of the items we were testing in adverse conditions. It was a primus, which worked with the aid of methylated spirit and would not blow out in a wind. It was easy to conceal from view and, unlike burning bracken and wood, produced little flame and literally no smoke, so was very handy in an enclosed space. It was also a means of warmth, which I found most useful in the atrociously cold weather.

We set off in groups of eight, our destination a compass bearing from a given map reference. In my group were Corporal Jackson, Jimmy Metcalfe, Harry Humphries, Chunky Coult, George Warner, Jim Crabtree and Lutner. It was misty and cold, with a yellow grey sky that signalled snow, and over the next few days we encountered every known weather condition: rain, hail, snow, gale-force winds, and even bright sunshine on the last day. With the aid of our special rations, string vests to retain warmth, and rifles with live ammunition, we got by. As we were on a fend-for-yourself endurance test, we took advantage of a deer that happened to pass by and shot it for food. On returning to camp there was a complaint from a local man about someone shooting his deer, but not much pressing was done to find the culprit. I must say, although only half-cooked, that meat went down very well with our tea.

Returning to Ringway, it was wonderful to get back to our comfortable digs, with piping hot meals prepared in a civilised manner. Our landladies were worth their weight in gold the way they looked after us, though we knew that, having passed the initial test of endurance, we could not afford to let ourselves get too floppy or over-confident.

The next thing was to be trained as parachutists and we began practising the art of landing without breaking any bones or knocking ourselves silly through landing awkwardly. I managed various ways of leaving moving and static objects, including jumping from a one-and-a-half-ton truck travelling at fifteen miles per hour, which is fast when you deliberately fall off. No one complained when this practice was abolished after too many bones got broken. But when was the real jumping going to start? 'When you can swing it properly, lad, and I don't mean the lead—most of you are good at that already!' Regimental Sergeant Major Mansie said. We had to practise again and again, and we were to find out why soon enough. It would be a matter of life or death when put to the real test.

The fuselage of a Whitley bomber was slung up in a fixed position in the hangar to enable us to practise emplaning. We had to shuffle down on our buttocks and gather round the gaping aperture. It was about the most uncomfortable form of travel the boffins at the War Office could have thought of. The parachute harness drill was a bit of a drag, but all-important. You would be 40 feet up on a platform in the roof of the hangar and the instructor would give you a tap on the shoulder as the signal to jump off. If you were a little slow he would give a gentle shove. That wasn't too bad, swinging back and forth two or three times, but then you were given the order to jump, at which you were to release yourself from the harness. You were 20 feet from the ground and had to gauge your swing as you hit the quick release box positioned on your chest. On the start of the forward swing, you would sharply push the harness off your shoulders and jump, hoping that you landed still with the forward movement and could then go into a side roll.

Next came our first jump out of 'Bessie', a static barrage balloon situated in Tatton Park, a few miles from Knutsford. The day was clear, fine, cloudless, and, fortunately, windless. Getting into the queue to draw my parachute, I hoped sincerely that the Women's Auxiliary Air Force packers had carried out the correct procedure. I didn't notice much on my way to the Park as my mind was too intent on jumping. Then the lorry came to a stop close to 'that thing'! The driver wished us well, pointing in the direction of the lake and saying, 'Don't drift into the drink—the owners won't like it'. It was all very well for him to joke, but I couldn't swim.

Waddling along to the balloon, trussed up like a chicken, I climbed into the cage for the first time and all the hangar training flashed through my mind. 'Hold tight!' shouted the RAF sergeant instructor. Then, with a whirr, the winch gave a jerk and up we started to go. I stared through the hole at the rapidly receding ground and wished myself back in the hangar at Ringway. The instructor shouted not to look down. 'Look up at Bessie!'

'Action stations! Ready, number one—go!' Number one went but I didn't notice. 'Number two!' rang in my ears. Jesus, that's me. Swinging my legs over into the hole, I gripped the side ready for the push off and it seemed like ages before the command 'Go'. When it did come, I don't remember leaving but I felt like I was in a vacuum, with cold air ripping at my face and legs. I was jerked violently like a rag doll as the chute obediently opened.

Looking up, Bessie was already quite some distance away. A voice shouted, 'Keep your bloody knees together and slightly bent, Curtis!' Then I hit the ground. I had made it! I managed to collapse my parachute and twist and undo the locking box to the harness, feeling so chuffed and thinking, 'I'm going to like this'. After Sid Oxley and Jim Parker had jumped, the balloon was winched down in readiness for the next four men: Chunky Coult, George Warner, Harry Humphries and Jimmy Metcalfe. Jimmy was the oldest among us at 32. He was nifty with his fists, being the Battalion flyweight boxer.

They climbed in with the jumpmaster and the balloon ('the ghost', we called it) was again winched up. Harry was to jump first, followed by George, Jimmy and Chunky. Harry went, but George somehow didn't like that claustrophobic, creaking cage, with its gaping hole to jump out through, and he didn't jump. On his return to

Ringway he was put on a charge, placed in an improvised cell in the guardroom and subjected to all sorts of military intimidation. It seemed to me that here was a man who had *volunteered* to take part and, though he did not come up to expectations on his first jump, how could such a man be put on a charge—especially when everyone else had yet to complete seven jumps from an aircraft in order to qualify for their wings and become parachutists? Word soon got around about poor George's plight, and so to the ears of William Connor, the newspaper columnist writing as 'Cassandra' in *The Daily Mirror*, who raised a stink with the war lords and somehow managed to get our George out of the nick. George did not become a Para but at least was returned to his parent regiment with no charges being brought. For my own part, I had made it. I had actually made it and I felt bloody good!

When I carried out my first jump from an aircraft, among my 'stick' of eight Paras were Corporal Law and Guardsmen Webster and Sambourne. We emplaned and settled down in the gloomy darkness—four of us straddled on each side of that gaping aperture. The two engines reverberated louder and louder, making my ears ring and crackle. As we gathered momentum, through the hole the runway looked like a lot of streaky lines, and then we were airborne. Approaching Tatton Park at around 2,000 feet, we circled, before dropping to a steady 800-foot run in. The butterflies started their tour of my insides as the instructor shouted, 'We're running in. Get ready!' The old Whitley reduced speed and seemed to hover. Cripes, I hope that pilot knows his job, I thought. If he reduces speed much more we'll drop out of the sky. 'Action stations, red light on!' With eyes glued to that light, hands stretched out on the floor, ready for the heave to the edge of the aperture, knees together and bent, I am sure that I froze. 'Green light—Go! One—Two—Three! That was me. Swinging to the point of no return on the edge, I pushed myself forward and, retaining the 'attention' position, out I went.

One second I had that rattle of engines in my ears and jumping orders were being rapped out, and the next there was a terrific *whoosh* as the slipstream caught up with me. Then I felt a sharp jerk. Looking up, only about 100 feet away the Whitley seemed so small already as it flew on towards Ringway. Sitting up here felt great. It was my first proper jump, the weather was just right, and the war was forgotten as I floated down. The last 100 feet did not feel quite so good as the ground came rushing up to meet me, then, *wham*. I rolled over to my left and came to a gentle stop while the parachute and rigging lines collapsed around me. Jumping up, I ran towards some other men and we all started congratulating one another. Someone called to me, 'I see you managed to ring the bell, Lofty!' ('Ring the bell' was the term used when you hit your nose on the side of the aperture upon leaving the aircraft.) Wiping my nose with the back of my hand, I saw that blood had been drawn. 'Who cares?' I shouted back. 'Who cares!' We began a brisk walk to the tea hut situated in a small copse of pine trees, singing to the strains of *John Brown's Body*: 'There was blood upon the harness, there was blood upon the chute; the paratrooper's intestines were hanging from his boots…' I hoped I didn't finish up that way. I was thinking that I was going to like parachuting, and now had just six jumps to go before being fully qualified.

Within the next week our seven jumps had been achieved and we could not wait to sew those blue wings on the right arm of the battledress blouse. One lad even brought his sewing kit along with him and sat down in a corner of the hangar to get them on before anyone else. It was odd to see men walking around in Wythenshawe and Manchester with their winged shoulders slightly forward of the rest of their bodies. Civilians and other non-Para soldiers were asking, 'Who are these blokes with wings—some sort of secret unit?'

Number 2 Commando had quite a share in the casualty list in these early days. One chap who had a lucky escape was Guardsman Frank Garlick, who became entangled by his static line and parachute under the belly of a Whitley. He couldn't release himself, so the RAF crew decided to get back to Ringway, called out the emergency services and hoped for the best. They landed with Frankie bumping around under the belly, and fire tenders, ambulances and personnel dashed with all speed to his aid. To the amazement of everyone, he just stepped out from under the aircraft, unlocked his parachute harness and calmly walked away, looking none the worse for the unusual landing.

We were training both as parachutists and also for the specialized work of the commando, which meant that a lot of extra work had to be put in to achieve the very best end-result. Above all, it was emphatically stressed that we should never accept defeat, even when up against overwhelming odds, and we were taught to persevere to the end and to be able to endure great, if not impossible, fatigue. Fortunately, to break the monotony of such intensive training, we were all encouraged to get out and about when off duty, with the emphasis on more enjoyable pastimes. A favourite haunt was the Benchill pub, where the landlord sometimes had a problem with us at closing time. We would have been much more cooperative if only he had not been so regimental. On one occasion when he was doing his best to get us out, Sam Coster, Frankie Thompson and a dozen others started to slowly sing the National Anthem, making everyone stop what they were doing and stand still as was customary. To our amusement and the landlord's annoyance, this was repeated several times.

In February, six Whitleys transported men of 'X' Troop in an operation codenamed 'Colossus', the first time men of our No. 2 Commando, 11th S.A.S. Battalion were used, and the first British parachute operation of the war. Their objective was to attack and destroy the Tragino aqueduct at Apulia in Italy. The operation, led by Major T.A.G. Pritchard, was a success insofar as five of the old Whitleys reached the target and the men managed to blow up the aqueduct. However, the Italian interpreter was killed and everyone else captured. Only Lieutenant Anthony Deane-Drummond, a signals officer, later escaped to fight another battle.

Chapter Four
Unorthodox Methods of Training

For a while we seemed to spearhead innumerable training schemes involving local Home Guard units and other military or civilian authorities. These were designed both to sharpen us up and to keep them on their toes. Once, it was night-time when we crept down from some woods to a convoy of thirty Army trucks and removed the distributors and the valves from all the tyres, which was as effective as destroying them in action. One of these vehicles was the ration truck, which, after overpowering a somewhat indignant quartermaster and sergeant, we nicked, complete with rations. The local Regular Army had no food for quite a while that day.

On another exercise, this time involving the whole of Southern Command, the drop zone was in the country area of Pilgrim's Way, between Harrietsham and Warren Street, eight miles from Maidstone in Kent. We took on the Home Guard at a crossroads. They were very enthusiastic and, with a yell, adopted the 'on guard' position with their rifles and rushed us. I had a .45 Colt in my hand as the nearest one came at me, lunging menacingly. I parried his action and a dismayed Home Guardsman was quickly looking down the barrel of his own rifle. Umpires standing by gave us the winning points. During this exercise one soldier in a scout car unfortunately got in the way of a blank fired from the rifle of one of our men, and even a blank can cause severe discomfort if you are too near the blast.

We played as much havoc with the civilian police. Seeing some Royal Military Police 'Redcaps' milling around a civil police station, we decided to shake them all up. Using a thunder flash and dummy grenades, we rushed the station and took it, informing the Redcaps they were dead too. We were then confronted by a rather put out police sergeant, complaining that we had made a mess of his station. 'Think yerself lucky we ain't real Germans', said a young cockney Para. Upon which, the umpires walked in and pronounced all the police stone dead and the station ours.

Another interesting scheme, involving a drop, was the capture of Norwich Castle. After the drop, everyone mustered in their respective troops and sections and we set off in various ways for the castle. My section of 'L' Troop, which included Guardsmen Butcher and Crabtree, decided to commandeer a bus. Turfing off the reluctant bus driver and conductor, who had to be forcibly removed, we lay low on the floor of the bus and sped a little faster through the town than a bus normally does. As it was not exactly a bus route we were on and half of Norwich would soon notice, we thought it best to change tactics. Dumping the bus, we made our way through back alleys, gardens and side roads to avoid the main road. Then our lead scout came belting back to inform us with delight that there was an unattended ambulance around the corner, just waiting to be used for something or other. What luck!

Randal, an Irish lad, slipped into the driver's seat while the rest of us opened the rear doors and made ourselves comfortable inside. He started the engine with a key left conveniently in position. 'Look sharp, Paddy', someone whispered as he fought with the gears—he'd only ever driven a tram before. As two dismayed ambulance men came running out of a building, we lurched forward and tore off, some of us adding insult to injury by giving the victory sign! We could not dally too long as the authorities would soon be on to us. More than once we were flagged down but simply drove on. After a while, the castle loomed a short distance away and I could see other members of our 'L' and 'H' Troops getting ready for the final assault. Captain Bromley-Martin was already at the gates with a section of 'L' Troop. Parking the ambulance in a side street, we doubled off to join the remainder unopposed. We took the Castle.

Back at Ringway we settled down to some experimental work with arms and equipment. Captain Tony Hibbert was eager to sort out an easier way to carry three-inch mortar bombs and devised a method of altering the pouch that was normally used to carry Bren gun magazines. We also developed some unusual military procedure for the use of the mortar in the event of the base-plate, barrel or sights being damaged in action or going astray on a supply drop. We found that with only the barrel the mortar could still be fired, provided that the man holding the barrel had gloves on and was strong. The ball pivot at the base of the barrel had to be set on firm ground, but not rock hard or the barrel would take off when fired and give anyone in the immediate vicinity a nasty knock. In soft ground a hole would soon appear and the procedure was to bung it up with a stone or anything hard at hand, repeating the process after firing each shell.

The fighting knife, which everyone prized and kept in perfect working order, was also found to be most useful for preparing meals and killing and gutting animals to replenish Army issue. In combat Paras had their own private places of concealment for quick and efficient delivery to the enemy, fixed either to the leg or belt, in the inside sleeve of the Airborne smock, or hidden between the neck of the smock and battle dress blouse. We practiced not only the use of the knife but also how best to avoid one when used against us.

Chinese experts taught us judo and unarmed combat. A rifle with fixed bayonet would be flung at you by the instructor, who would yell, 'Come on, lunge at me!' I lunged hesitantly the first time. 'Come on, Longshanks, lunge! You won't get anywhere near me!' Right, mate, I thought—you asked for it—and I took a really good lunge. But this man was an old hand. Like lightning, he parried my blow and before I knew it I was flat on my back, minus rifle. It was the same with the fighting knife, and quite a few of us nursed cuts at the end of a day's training. Those knives were razor-sharp.

In April of 1941 we were visited by Winston Churchill, accompanied by Sir Arthur Barratt and Major-General Sir Hastings Ismay. Each of us was eager to display his skills to the utmost and Churchill, wrapped in his overcoat, with trademark hat and stick, keenly watched several demonstrations. I was on unarmed combat with Sam Coster. When the Prime Minister ventured our way we put a little more realistic effort into it, much to my misfortune. Our prior arrangement was for Sam to throw me after I lunged at him with my knife. Sam parried my thrust, knocked the knife flying and obliged the Prime Minister with the best throw anyone had carried out for ages, flinging me hard on my back, my right arm taking my 14-stone weight. 'Go easy. I'm not a Jerry', I said, while Churchill looked on with a twinkle in his eye, as pleased as Punch. 'Did you try, lad?' he asked, stepping closer. 'What do you bloody think, Sir?' I blurted out. He pursed his lips, gave a big grin and waddled off looking delighted. I felt the after-effects of that throw for days.

Bypassing usual military procedure, various unorthodox methods in the use of small arms explosives were adopted and official eyes were shut so long as the end result was achieved. One such stunt was to withdraw the safety pin from a hand grenade, release the arm—which in turn would fire the four-second fuse in the primed grenade, making it really live—hold it for a second, and then throw it quickly, the object being to make sure the enemy would have no time to throw it back. Anyone refusing this dangerous venture would be subjected to a variety of flowery names. Luckily we had no casualties as a result.

Another method of firing the rifle was developed which enabled us to fire at almost the speed of a machine gun. To do so, when the first shot had been fired the bolt was not pushed home and locked in place and, therefore, flew open. Then, partially closing the bolt again and simultaneously pressing the trigger with the middle finger, another shot was fired. After a time, it was like a circular motion with the thumb, middle finger and palm of the hand. Although looking a little gangster-like, this was very effective as rapid fire. More than once the method would be used in North Africa and I'm sure the quickness of the action saved many a soldier.

For a while we had a change of scenery and went to an area of Hull made derelict by enemy bombing, and which offered good surroundings for a gruelling experience under live ammunition fire. Marksmen would fire Bren guns and rifles as near to us as they dared, and it was so like battle conditions that we could not avoid real casualties. At least this provided handy practice for the medics. Live hand grenades were issued and were to be thrown at given targets marked 'Grenade' as they appeared. As long as the grenade was aimed correctly and you dived for cover, all was well. Next, we played around with explosive booby traps in the derelict houses, using instantaneous fuses, orange in colour—the normal slow burning fuses being black. The explosive of detonator in guncotton could be set off by a trip wire attached to a trigger mechanism or by a pencil device that, when crushed, released an acid which burnt through a thin strand of copper wire. It only took a few seconds for the main charge to be detonated and it was quite tricky trying to locate these traps, feeling carefully and neutralizing them.

We were soon on the move once more, this time from our base at Ringway to a quiet place about ten miles away called Knutsford—quiet until we arrived, that is. I shared my digs with Corporal Hutson, another Guardsman, who later went off to train as an officer at Sandhurst. In fact, several of my friends finished up as commissioned officers, including Sergeant David Burwash who became a lieutenant in the 3rd Battalion and Sergeant Richard Bingley who became a captain with 'S' Company, 1st Para. Another lad, reluctant to be commissioned as the job was thought to be non-combatant, was Sergeant Harry Hutchins who was made officer and quartermaster more or less against his will by our commanding officer Colonel Down.

To keep on top form, we had plenty of physical training, cross country runs, compass marches and night exercises. Discipline was self-imposed and any need to impose it by a superior was frowned upon. Psychological and physical resistance were driven to the utmost until men could take their limit and even more, but it was never enough. We were marched, counter-marched and marched again in fair weather and in foul. Live ammunition fired at close range actually helped—I found myself so preoccupied with making sure I did not get hit that I became oblivious to fatigue and plodded on. At the end of a day's training I would stretch out on the hangar floor absolutely shagged. On passing, Sergeant Sid Oxley might prod me and say something like, 'Not bad lad, not bad. Do better tomorrow, eh?' 'Get stuffed' was the usual quiet reply as I slipped a well-earned cigarette between my lips and drew hard.

Apart from the Whitley, other types of aircraft used for training were the Halifax, Wellington and Albermarle. During this period we carried out jumps from Wellingtons and Whitleys day and night. The jumpmaster would call for anyone wishing to go for a flip to look sharp and sign for a chute. In a 'pull off' jump from a Whitley the drill was to hang on for dear life to the bar in the rear gun-turret housing and, after the cord was pulled, the parachute would open and you were literally pulled off. You would get corns on your backside and metal splinters in your hands through skidding along the floor in a sitting position. Such were the discomforts of early parachute training. But Flight Sergeant Brereton, Regimental Sergeant Major Mansie and Sergeant Dawes were fine instructors and we had such confidence in them that I'm sure we'd have jumped without parachutes if they'd assured us we'd be all right.

The packing of parachutes was mostly carried out by a team from the Women's Auxiliary Air Force, under Flight Sergeant Humphries. Every time a drop was in progress they really worried in case any had not been packed correctly. They were wonderful girls, those WAAFs. Initially, we had packed our own chutes. It was quite a straightforward job but the practice ceased as soon as it started, as the idea was only to give us confidence in their function.

A bag was attached to the parachute harness, which was carried on the back. The parachute was housed in an internal bag divided into two parts. One part remained attached to the harness, while the other was pulled violently from it by the static line attached to the inner bag. At the other end a 'D' ring engaged a hook attached to the end of a strop, which in turn was securely anchored to the aircraft. The canopy of the parachute was made of nylon or cotton, having a diameter of 28 feet and a vent at the apex 20 inches in diameter, which helped to reduce strain and oscillation. Together with rigging lines and static line, there were some 35 feet between you and the plane after the parachute had opened.

On one jump into Tatton Park, carried out from a Whitley with seven other Guardsmen from 'L' Troop, things did not quite go to plan. In the air over the Park the old Whitley began to splutter and lose height. The instructor shouted, 'Hold tight!' and before anyone could ask any questions we were making a bumpy belly landing, fortunately on the grass, missing the trees and lake by a good margin. We were quickly ushered out, bundled on to a troop carrier and whisked back to Ringway to immediately board another plane. Then it was back to Tatton Park for the drop, which this time went well for us. One of the jumpers, Lieutenant Stanley Wandless, joined me and Peter Sambourne afterwards on our way to the tea hut and said he wondered if that first run was a ploy of the C.O. to see how we would react in an emergency.

Lieutenant-Colonel Eric Down, known by the lads as 'Dracula', had taken command of the Battalion at around the time that Germany attacked the Soviet Union in June 1941. No one could find a good word for him at first, though I must say that anything we could do he could often do better, and I liked his enthusiastic way. He would have no quibbles at the thought of joining us on a scheme or setting the pace at the head of a column on a 100-mile route march. During his tenure, in September 1941, the name of the Battalion was changed once again and we now became the 1st Parachute Battalion. More battalions were raised and soon we were part of the 1st Parachute Brigade. Unfortunately, Colonel Down never took us into action because he left to establish the 2nd Parachute Brigade before we had that opportunity.

Pilot Officer Arthur Nutter, with others of the RAF, did a great job in getting us on target during our training drops in Tatton Park and Ringway. Some accidents were unavoidable but we had to learn the hard way. After becoming efficient parachutists, capable of dropping anywhere under any conditions and able to quickly get our bearings, we started to carry out further advanced experiments. One problem was how best to deliver arms and ammunition, as the parachutist is helpless without these being supplied in quantity. There were many hash-ups, with wireless equipment being damaged on landing, or the lid of a container getting jammed upon sharp impact with the ground, which would be a serious problem when you needed a weapon in a hurry.

A new container was designed to take heavy equipment, with bricks and sandbags used in place of stores in the early stage of testing, but it just would not work right. Not only did the bottom of the container fall out, the small lights on the side of the base, a must for quick identification at night, went out upon impact with the ground. In time, a version was produced which did the job and could carry anything from mortars and mortar bombs to Bren guns and wireless sets. The containers were fixed under the belly of the aircraft and dropped between set numbers of parachutists while they were jumping, the drill being: 'Go! One—Two—Three—Four—Container—Five—Six—Seven—Eight—Container...' The men jumping as numbers five and nine would be forewarned to allow for the containers to go.

Someone thought up a way for a man to carry his own supplies from the plane. I was not keen on this at first as it was bad enough having the parachute on, together with small arms and other gear. I had become used to that but now I also had to have a big kitbag strapped to my leg with 20 feet of rope attached to the bag and secured to my belt. After jumping, the kitbag was released from the leg by a quick-release knot and then down it went to land before the parachutist. This enabled extra supplies of up to 100 pounds to accompany each man.

Many days were spent in the hanger at Ringway and I knew every inch of it and everybody there. One day, Crabtree, Lawton, Sam Coster, Lieutenant Bolitho, Pat O'Brien and Cadwallader were in a group practising unarmed combat, while I was trying out 'the Gallows' with Stanley Wandless, Tommy Hughes and Jimmy Metcalfe. This involved jumping from the full height of about 40 feet from the Whitley's belly on to a gym mat—just one more unsuitable method used to practice landing, which was later abolished as more men were getting injured using it than when jumping from an aircraft. A group of unknowns ventured through the hangar doorway. 'Strangers in the house', someone called. One of the strangers was a Major John Frost, later to become very well known within the Airborne forces.

We got on extremely well with all ranks of the RAF. This parachuting work was a new baby to them and they were most keen and obliging in every way. On an evening out it would be quite normal to see a couple of Para privates and an officer having a beer and chatting with an RAF sergeant instructor. My parent Guards Regiment would have frowned upon such conduct as most unbecoming and prejudicial to good discipline, but in our case the discipline was there without the bull.

To keep the Royal Air Force on its toes our training in shock methods was also used with them as our target. On one such exercise in Lancashire, with an airfield as our main objective, Sam Coster and Chunky Coult found they had been dropped a few miles short of the main body of assault troops. In the dark they saw a telephone box with an RAF lad inside making a call, while conveniently parked close by was his motor-bike and sidecar. As he opened the door he saw Chunky sitting in the sidecar and Sam planted one on him with that big fist of his, leaving him nursing a sore chin as they roared away on the bike. A hazardous journey ensued through villages and the dark Lancashire countryside, busting through roadblocks on the way, Chunky flinging off fused gun cottons with detonators and producing some lively explosions. Even if live ammunition could not be used, we went as near as damn it to the real thing!

During a raid on another airfield my troop was to attack the hangars, and to do so a sentry post on the outer perimeter had to be silenced. A road ran from the post to scattered aircraft and we wanted to use transport captured from the Regular Army a few miles back to dash along the road and deal with those aircraft. Two Paras rushed the sentries and declared them 'dead'. One of the sentries obviously thought that dead men could still make phone calls and made to lift the telephone, so one of our men produced his fighting knife and slashed through the telephone wire. A rather indignant Air Force man was told again, 'You're dead, mate. Dead!' The two Paras pushed the barrier open and the rest of us belted through in our captured trucks. Fanning out as we went, we could hear a commotion over the rest of the airfield as everyone did their job. My section, comprising three men, had to attack a hangar west of the control tower, while others gave covering fire. We threw our guncotton bombs into the hangar and withdrew sharply. The resultant noise in that lofty hangar was gigantic! With all the blanks being fired, thunder flashes going off, and the occasional short-fused guncotton producing quite a blast, the Air Force probably thought we were the real enemy. After the exercise everyone spoke of the bewilderment and surprise caused by the speed of our attack and withdrawal.

On this occasion we didn't use the Gammon bomb, as that would have been a little too powerful. Lieutenant R.J. Gammon, who was always tinkering around with explosives, had invented this weapon. One day he put the wind up me by tossing one in my direction and calling out, 'Here, catch', which I did very gingerly, though of course it was not primed. The bomb consisted of plastic explosive, gun cotton and detonator, the whole being placed in a black cotton bag with an elastic top. We practiced the use of these against rock faces in the Lancashire hills, where, after half a dozen terrific blasts, they cracked the rock. They later proved most useful in action for knocking out tanks and pillboxes.

Another exercise, put on especially for the benefit of the national press, was in the form of an attack on a farm building. My section was to defend the farm. We waited for the attack for a long while in the damp, cold morning dew. A handful of pressmen were there with all their paraphernalia to study and report on the new type of fighting soldier. I had seen them before with their special passes at Ringway, and in a plane too, clicking away with their cameras. A cry went out from our sentry, 'Stand by! Enemy approaching!' Cocking our rifles, loaded with blanks for realism, we took up our positions. I could see small shapes moving in the undergrowth and nipping past gaps in the hedgerow. Then I heard the cough of a two-inch mortar, signalling the delivery of smoke bombs. Small arms fire began cracking away and the whole area was enveloped in smoke. The attackers burst through the haze and I could make out Sergeant Jim Bushnell and Jimmy Metcalfe, followed closely by other yelling Paras. The attack was over in no time, but we had our lesson in soldiering and there were plenty of photographs for the press, so everyone went off pleased with the results.

During one display staged at Ringway for yet more government officials and generals, a sudden wind got up. We nevertheless took off in six Whitleys, circled and came in to drop. Leaving the aircraft was fine, but I felt a cold breeze lapping my face and weather conditions were quite dismal. At 100 feet I was drifting and oscillating like mad, and by 40 feet it was even worse and butterflies were popping around inside me. In the last 20 feet I thought of all my past training. I was hoping for an upward swing backward, so that on the last swing forward I could go into a roll and correct the inevitable rough landing, but, alas, no. I was only about three feet from the ground on that forward swing, putting my plan in reverse, and I landed half on my back and shoulders, while at the same time my knees were forced into my chest. Partly knocked out, I finished up being dragged 400 yards before some RAF men pounced and collapsed my chute for me. I came to in an ambulance on the way to Daveyhulme Hospital in Manchester, where I had to remain for a week, though it did make a pleasant change, what with pretty nurses hopping around and doing things for me. Then I had another week of recovery back at my digs. Well, it had to happen sometime. Parachuting was a dangerous business.

Our uniform was getting more uniform now. Gone was the chocolate-coloured headgear made of canvas, with a rubber band sown inside to protect the head on landing. In its place we had a steel helmet similar to that of the German parachutist, which later proved to be rather problematic because we were mistaken for the enemy on more than one occasion in Africa. The first jumping smock had been a light gabardine, whereas the new issue was thicker and camouflaged in mottled brown, green and yellow. The first jumping boots had been black with laced sides to prevent injury on heavy landing, and thin rubber soles. These were replaced with standard-type Army boots, though still with rubber soles. On the whole, the uniform and gear were getting better.

In March of 1942 we moved to Bulford on Salisbury Plain in Wiltshire, where we were housed in Kiwi

Barracks, our home and base for the next six months. It felt strange to again hear *Reveille*, *Lights Out* and many other calls being blasted out on the bugle, but I soon became re-accustomed to the rigours of barrack life—my first time since 1939 in Aldershot at the start of the war. We even had the occasional drill parade to keep those reflexes on top form. We were honoured with a visit by King George VI and Queen Elizabeth and our unit must have commanded some respect as we were asked to put on a show. As usual, the weather was awful, but everything went off OK. I remember thinking that the King looked a little weary. After two-and-a-half years of war I suppose everyone was.

My 1st Battalion was still upset at missing out on the Bruneval Raid, which in February had successfully destroyed a German radar installation near Le Havre in northern France. Our 2nd Battalion, under Major John Frost, had that pleasure. The disastrously unsuccessful raid on Dieppe in August was another that we all trained for, but at the last moment were taken off. Actually, the Battalion grew quite accustomed to cancellations and as a result the atmosphere became rather tense in the Bulford and Salisbury area. Men of all units were getting worked up to a pitch, knowing that at any time they could be going into action, and the prolonged inactivity led to friction all round.

In August our 1st Parachute Brigade had officially become part of what was now the Parachute Regiment. Troops with red berets were appearing in greater numbers in the district, and for the first time we met up with members of the Airborne Signals Regiment, together with men from the 1st Parachute Squadron, Royal Engineers, who would later prove invaluable to us in North Africa and Sicily. A troop of the Royal Engineers was to be attached to my Battalion and we all soon became firm friends. That special *esprit de corps* was beginning to take a really good hold now between us Airborne men. Other regiments in the area could be very inquisitive about our quality as extra-tough fighting men and sometimes sought to find out the hard way. Quite a few of our lads came back after a night on the beer nursing bloody noses and black eyes. But of course they always said the other blokes got the worst of it!

There were night exercises, which mainly involved finding our way back to camp with a given compass bearing. We would climb into a lorry and, with flaps drawn, tour an area in ever increasing circles, giving the impression that we had travelled a great distance, when in fact we had only gone a couple of miles. These exercises always took place on very dark nights when there were no stars or moonlight to illuminate known landmarks. On one such night even the compasses were withdrawn, so I thought of past training and of how the moss always forms on the north side of a tree. If you were up on local geography you could soon find your way back to base. To encourage more enthusiasm, packets of cigarettes and beer were hidden at certain points and, provided with map references, we would all set off to secure the reward before the next man. This made us get a move on while testing our skill in getting around unaided.

Sam and I thought we would like to sample a day in London and after a bit of a wangle we acquired the necessary passes and made off. Everywhere we went it cost a fortune to enjoy ourselves and in no time our meagre pay was seriously diminished. Working our way around Piccadilly and the Strand to Trafalgar Square, we encountered two Redcaps at the foot of one of those big lions who appear to be on the lookout for the unexpected incident. We were approached by the corporal, a regimental-looking so-and-so with not a stitch out of place. 'Your passes', he snapped. I looked at Sam. Sensing a little game, we tapped our battledress blouse pockets and felt our trousers. 'Had it somewhere', I said. 'Can't find it anywhere', said Sam. 'I know—can we leave our address? Will that be OK? Seem to have mislaid the silly thing'. We watched the corporal unbutton his pocket in anticipation of pinching two para-commandos and, when his book was in hand and pencil poised ready for action, both said with great surprise, 'Ah, here it is—in the field service dressing pocket!' After very close scrutiny our passes were reluctantly returned and the two Redcaps moved off, looking most disappointed at not nailing us.

We crossed the road to a pub opposite the Horse Guards entrance in Whitehall and adopted the usual stance, elbow supporting the bar. Awaiting some service, Sam pulled out his wallet, a ten-shilling note and a pound note covering what looked like many more English notes. I knew the drill—it had worked before and why not again? I ordered two pints from the barmaid, a well-developed girl with a tight-fitting black skirt and shapely legs sunk into high-heeled shoes. She wore one of those short-sleeved pink crocheted tops with large holes, but small enough to make you fix your gaze to ascertain whether or not she had anything on underneath. A few inches from where that full bosom was gently swelling and heaving, I hoisted myself up on two elbows and, with a little flattery, gave her some small talk while Sam said, 'How much, love?' He slipped a note over the bar, which being cluttered, and with all the distracting chat, she didn't notice was not an English one. 'Oh, and twenty Players, please.' Compliments still flying, the unsuspecting girl picked up the note and gave change for a pound. We enjoyed our pints and cigarettes, and before leaving ordered 'one for the road'. 'Cheers!' I said to Sam. 'Down the hatch!' he replied. 'Vive La France! Vive La France!' Well, that was one way of getting rid of left over 100 Franc notes.

The 1st Parachute Brigade carried out numerous lengthy exercises, all the time keeping us to a high peak of fitness through physical training, cross-country runs and unarmed combat. We conducted one exercise with 2 Para near Exford in Somerset. I remember Tony Lucas of 'T' Company passing some remark about 'donkey men' when I came by with a trolley loaded with three-inch mortar gear. 'Get lost!' was my polite reply of the day. Live ammunition was used and we all tried to make ourselves as small as possible when the mortars started coughing and Bren guns rattling.

Another way to get us used to being under fire was to make us crawl in a hollow in the ground while marksmen let fly as near as they dared. If your rear was up too far it was soon lowered at the first burst of Bren fire. Then a 'Stop!' notice would loom up in front and someone would let fly a hand grenade. After the *crump* and whine of segregated pieces of metal as they passed by, an 'All Clear' notice would appear and the order to continue advancing on the enemy position be given.

Our hopes of getting into action were raised once more in September when we trained for an attack upon the island of Ushant, just off the coast of Brittany. It was to be more or less a training exercise, though this time with the real enemy. By now, Lieutenant-Colonel James Ledger Hill was our 1st Battalion C.O. and the mission was to be carried out in cooperation with 2 Para, commanded by Lieutenant-Colonel Geoffrey Gofton-Salmond. But once again the operation was cancelled.

The previous 21 months of experimental work had I think been worthwhile, as we had become an efficient force, and one to be reckoned with. We had come a long way since those first batches of volunteers in 1940. Our 1st Parachute Battalion had grown into a regiment, and as well as the wings on the right sleeve of our battledress, we also wore the Pegasus badge—Bellerophon (the hero and slayer of monsters of Greek mythology) astride a winged horse, with cloak fluttering in the wind and brandishing a spear.

At this time, Dakota transport aircraft of the United States Army Air Force began to arrive in the area and we met up with the American 502nd Parachute Infantry Regiment troops who were stationed at Hungerford, about 25 miles from our own camp. I found them a good lot of men, always ready to show off their parachuting technique like old hands. They wondered how on earth we had managed with a Whitley. One remarked, 'Gee, buddy, you must've got doggone cramp!' The new way of leaving an aircraft was much better, I must say, as we soon got into the swing of jumping from two types of Dakota—the C47 and C53. The C47 had an almost square door opening and, being over six-foot-two, I preferred this to the smaller C53 with its oval top, which I invariably hit when making my exit. And so it was goodbye to the Whitley and Wellington as far as dropping troops was concerned.

Strong rumours now began to circulate in the camps of an intended move to an unspecified battlefront and the prospect of getting to grips with the enemy became our main topic of conversation. In the NAAFI, in the washrooms, in the guardroom, even in the privacy of the loo, there was the constant hum of men chatting with great enthusiasm about the possible places we could be going to. At last, our hopes of a move were rewarded when the 1st Parachute Brigade received orders for mobilization and overseas service. The atmosphere was one of almost jubilation. This was to be the last time that the whole Brigade would be together in close proximity before travelling and fighting as individual units.

Chapter Five
A Cruise to North Africa

After saying farewell to Kiwi Barracks we made our way to Greenock in the west of Scotland, where to our great surprise at the quayside lay a massive collection of shipping. The Brigade was allotted two troopships, mine being the *Arundel Castle,* which had been used for holiday cruises before the war, although it was somewhat cramped on this trip and without the luxury trimmings. I boarded, and after endless trudging along narrow passageways and up and down steep stairs and gangways, was directed to an area below the waterline, aft of the ship. Soon after casting off we learned that we were heading for Algiers, from where we would take part in a combined operation by Great Britain and the United States, codenamed 'Operation Torch'.

We had a safe journey, but going through the Bay of Biscay was rough and nearly everyone was seasick. I had more than my share and reckon I was continuously sick for four days and nights. I just didn't know where to put myself. But I got over it when the going became steadier and improved weather conditions enabled us to spend more time up top. In between physical training and regular boat-drills, it was interesting to watch our convoy of some 40 ships, including Royal Navy escorts, looking like toys dotted as far as the horizon. The escort ships were most active, darting among the merchantmen like sheep dogs mustering their flocks. It was comforting and good for morale to see them firing their 'multiple hedgehog' mortar depth charges, giving any German U-boats something to think about.

At length the Moroccan city of Tangiers came into view, its lights blazing away unconcernedly in the Mediterranean night sky. As we passed by there seemed no fear of war there and I wondered if they knew we were on our way to fight in Algeria. After an 11-day sea voyage everyone was more than pleased when we did finally reach Algiers. Looking down into the clear blue water as I waited to disembark, I saw some large mauve blobs, which must have been 18 inches across. 'Jelly fish', someone said, 'real stingers'. We waited for quite a while before managing to get ashore with our feet firmly clomped on the quayside. It was now the 12th of November and the sun was as hot as on an English midsummer's day.

We didn't hang around for long and were soon marching off through the outskirts of the city, singing and whistling. I was struck by the scruffiness of the locals, whose clothes were torn and tattered. Last year's dirt still seemed wrapped around their necks. The smell in the streets was awful and a cry of 'Blimey, what a stink!' came from the ranks. I felt glad to have been born and bred in England. Soon, we reached the clean fresh air of the open country and at last our destination, the aerodrome at Maison-Blanche.

We knew we were going somewhere to do a job but didn't know where or when. At Maison-Blanche we prepared for this long-awaited action. The time factor was the killer as usual, although there was plenty to do in preparation for our journey into the unknown: bombing-up containers, checking equipment, making sure that every detail was in order—arms and ammunition, field dressings, maps and rations. The iron ration was a highly concentrated chocolate in a sealed tin, only to be opened for consumption on the orders of an officer or if the situation was such that you were on your own, in which case you were to use as necessary. It was horrible stuff but saved the day on many occasions.

On the 15th of November we drew our parachutes and waited in the hangar, everyone getting a little restless. My shoulders were aching like anything with the tight-fitting parachute harness. Then someone shouted, 'On your feet, we're off!' 'Hoo-bloody-ray. About time', said Freddy Martin. The weather prospects were poor, and once we were airborne it was raining quite hard, forcing us to return to the aerodrome after about an hour and a half. Although we returned to a nice hot meal, the delay was another disappointment. At 11.00 the next morning we emplaned again. This time the weather looked good and there would be no cancellation. Everyone was wishing us luck.

We were informed that our objective was an enemy emergency airstrip, close to a place called Souk-el-Arba in Tunisia. Along the way we were attacked by two Me 109s, but these were successfully shot down by our escort of Spitfires. Thanks to the Americans easing their rule about smoking on aircraft I managed to feel more relaxed by puffing through half-a-dozen cigarettes. It was a three-hour journey in a very hot and humid heat and we sat in the plane sweating like pigs, singing songs and cracking jokes to try and hide our feelings. Chunky said, 'Well, Lofty, it won't be long now. See you in Heaven'. 'You must be joking, mate,' I replied tersely. 'He's got to be a damn good Jerry to catch up with me!' Then the order was bellowed out: 'Action stations!' It made me shiver. 'Hook up!' I was sweating like hell and felt a bit weak at the knees. I wondered out loud, 'What sort of a reception are we going to get?' 'What, mate?' Crabtree asked. 'Oh nothing', I muttered. I hooked up my line with shaky fingers, managing to endure ten minutes standing while the plane came in to drop us at this airfield out in the wilds, 70 miles from Tunis.

The jumpmaster's piercing voice cut through the sound of the aircraft: 'Stand to the door!' I swallowed hard and prepared for the exit. When the order to go rang in my ears I became a changed man—it suddenly felt so much cooler being whisked about in the air. All around me were hundreds of parachutes. We were finally dropping into action. I landed OK. Chunky was all right, and so were Sambourne, Pat O'Brien and Bill (Scratcher) Renwick. I saw Sam a hundred feet away, and Bill Shannon from Battalion HQ. Stanley Wandless had his pipe out already—maybe he didn't want to damage it on landing and had kept it firmly in his hand as he dropped. Sadly, one parachute had not functioned properly and the Para was killed, our very first casualty. He was Guardsman Webster, a friend of mine.

The drop was unopposed, except for some rather excitable Arabs who galloped towards us on frisky-looking horses. The riders wore flowing robes and brandished their long slender rifles like something out of a film set. They fired a few shots in the air, but in jubilation rather than hostility. We did not know at the time that the French troops and Tunisian Tirailleurs at Beja, Sidi Nsir and Oued Zarga were in two minds as to whether they should come and join us or go to the aid of the Germans. They had apparently had their guns trained on us, but fortunately no one was trigger-happy. Not far away, a German reconnaissance patrol gave us a quick look and then went off in the direction of Mateur. We managed to get organized and hide our parachutes, some being collected up by the Arabs on horseback, before a German fighter plane came to investigate. Then, with the American flag flying, we made our way into Souk-el-Arba, where we managed to commandeer enough Tunisian buses to transport the whole Battalion on to our next objective, the town of Beja. The French troops and African natives were cheering loudly with wild excitement, apparently happy with the invaders.

It was dark when we arrived just outside Beja. Getting out of the buses, the Battalion spread out, kipping down after posting sentries. The night was very cold among the rocks and sandy waste and when morning came I saw a vast expanse of wilderness stretching out around me. The rest of the Brigade would have witnessed similar sights, as Lieutenant-Colonel Frost led 2 Para in a drop at Depienne, some 40 miles south-east, and 3 Para, under Lieutenant-Colonel Pine-Coffin, dropped 100 miles north-west at Bone. With our 1st Battalion in the centre, there was thus a distance of about 140 miles between the three Battalions. This whole area was to be our home and battleground for the next five-and-a-half months.

As day dawned, the outline of an average-size tent could be seen across the hard dirt road. Beja lay asleep and all was quiet as I scanned the landscape. Then a sound came from the tent and out tumbled a gigantic Arab, complete with flowing robe and headgear, his sandals showing dirty great feet. He made an excitable remark, pulling and prodding at the tent opening, from where next came two women, followed by four shoeless children dressed in shabby long garments. And that was not all. Out stepped a donkey, wagging its tail before having a pee, then two scruffy dogs, snarling at each other's heels until brought to order by a fierce kick from the big Arab. To complete the cast, out came four large mice, or desert rats, much to the delight of the dogs, eager for a quick snack. At this point, the Arab cupped his hands to his mouth, the sound echoing around the surrounding hills as he bellowed, 'Who-oooh-Mohamed! Who-oooh-Mohamed!' The lads really liked this cry, and from then on we adopted it as the Para battle cry when assaulting enemy positions. The whole Brigade must have heard Arab men making this call, as it caught on not only here with 1st Battalion but with 2 and 3 Para too.

The Germans had left Beja, warning the French that if we came into town they would bomb it. Well, we marched through, and unfortunately the Germans kept their word and the town was almost flattened by Stuka bombers. Prior to our advance, some of the French troops were rather reluctant to face the enemy. We had met them on their retreat from Beja as we were advancing towards it. Colonel Hill had ordered them to turn about and come along with us, and Major Alastair (Jock) Pearson had persuaded them to comply with a drawn pistol. 'Les Boches, les Boches', they protested. 'So what', said one of our boys, 'We've come a long way to meet 'em. Come on—git!' Still protesting, they joined us.

I was posted to three-inch mortars and accompanied a reconnaissance patrol to the area of Sidi Nsir and Mateur. Our second-in-command Major Cleasby-Thompson was in charge of the patrol, made up of men from 'R' Company, including Lieutenant Philip Mellor and Company Sergeant Major Sammy Steadman. Forward scouts reported enemy transport ahead and we set an ambush and waited, our mortar positioned on a small hill. The German transport appeared after a while, and then everything let rip: mines, mortars, small arms fire and Gammon bombs. I heard a number of yells and screams, and in the open ground to the right of the ambush saw a movement. It looked like an English Airborne smock. Another yell came from the spot: 'Help. I've been hit!' It sounded like Sammy Steadman. Then I saw his profile. Yes, it was Sammy—there was no mistaking that give-away nose of his. He'd been hit in the leg. The bag was pretty good on this first big clash with the enemy and included German maps, Luger pistols, Zeiss field glasses and one undamaged scout car out of a mixed assortment of six.

We returned to Beja, where we had to put up with a couple of days of concentrated Stuka attacks. To bluff the Germans via their very gullible Arab informers, the Battalion was formed up, stretched out as far as possible and marched around the town to give the impression of far greater numbers. The ruse worked, not only fooling the enemy but also winning over the French in terms of their confidence in us. Leaving behind the somewhat dazed population of Beja, we then headed off in our commandeered buses in the direction of Medjez-el-Bab and Tunis.

We were machine-gunned constantly. One minute we were in the buses and the next taking cover. Once, with Pat Dolan and Chunky, I dashed for safety across open ground and slid into a hollow 100 feet from the dirt road as three small specks of Messerschmitts came diving straight for us from 4,000 feet. I lay on my stomach, looking at the aircraft through my camouflage net scarf as they came in fast. Much closer now, and the three of them opened fire, one concentrating on the road transport, the other two on our men scrambling for cover on each side of the road. Bullets slashed the ground ten feet from us, kicking up fountains of dust. 'Bloody hell, Pat, that was close', said Chunky. They circled and came in for another run, this time really low, only about fifty feet from the ground. A couple of our ack-ack guns let fly, Jerry let rip, and muck seemed to be flying everywhere—mainly rock splinters and dust. As one aircraft clattered by, I saw quite plainly the pilot with a white scarf around his neck. 'You f...ing fool. You might have killed us!' someone shouted, and then let out a bellowing laugh. Amazingly, after all that strafing, no one was seriously hurt and only two of our vehicles were rendered unserviceable.

As time went on, things continued to hot up and the buses were soon abandoned in favour of footslogging. It was dark when we arrived at the small hamlet of Oued Zarga, where I would spend the next few days dug in with Scratcher Renwick, Crabtree, Pat and Chunky. The local French troops and Tunisian Tirailleurs had a handful of men here, as they had also at Medjez-el-Bab and Sidi Nsir, and our presence boosted their morale, which was just as well considering that they had been thinking of throwing in their lot with the Germans. Fortunately, the soil in this desolate area made for fairly easy digging and I was soon to realise the comparative security of my slit trench.

It was around noon, the sun was hot and my shirt was wet through with sweat. The atmosphere was clammy in more ways than one as Jerry acclimatised himself to the fact that we were here to stay, most probably in force. We would shortly experience his fighting quality, together with more of his air strike ability. On receiving an air raid warning from Wally Boldock, our vigilant sentry, I dived for my slit trench. Collecting myself, I looked around at the disappearing posteriors of other Paras seeking safety in their own holes in the ground. The drone of aircraft could now be heard and the moving black spots came into clearer view, crossing my front. I slowly drew my scarf over my face and peered through the square mesh, hypnotized by those moving spots, which were getting ever larger and nearer. Then they turned towards us—three Stuka dive-bombers—approaching at about 5,000 feet. The sky was clear and visibility was good. It was most weird not knowing whether they were interested in us or were just passing. But they were interested in us all right. The leading pilot made a half roll and nosed down, the preliminary to commencing that awe-inspiring Stuka dive at an angle of 85 degrees.

As it whined nearer, I could see the evil gull-winged shape so clearly. It seemed to be approaching me head-on and I was at my wits' end as to whether I should get out and run for it or stay put and possibly perish. Before I could make up my mind, I saw four black dots moving away from the aircraft. They were bombs, seemingly aimed directly at me, their descent accompanied by a high-pitched scream. I gripped my smock and braced myself. The sides of my slit trench shook and a shower of freshly dug soil cascaded over my face, partly filling the trench. 'Christ, that's close', I thought out loud. The other two Stukas came in to repeat the treatment and there seemed to be a never-ending succession of bombs violently vibrating the ground. Then the drone of aircraft drifted away and, as black smoke billowed slowly skyward, voices began to ring out as men sought reassurance that others were OK. Chunky was there on the edge of my trench, asking if I was all right. Putting on a brave front, I said I was, and I was except for a little excretion. But then getting away with nothing more than wet pants after that lot did not hurt my pride. I didn't tell the others, though.

For the rest of that day we were unmolested by aircraft, but from then on there were plenty of patrol skirmishes in company lines both day and night as German paratroopers were busy in the area. Our positions were on a rise, just above a secondary dirt road running through some cacti and brush, and there were a few isolated trees looking the worse for the past aerial bombing. The road twisted round this rock-strewn desert landscape to link up a short distance away with the Beja to Medjez-el-Bab road.

One morning, as the commotion of war eased towards dawn, the results of the previous night's fighting gradually became visible. I could make out a motionless form in the track 150 yards ahead of me in the dip where the road snaked between cacti and rocks. And there was another laying very still to the right. I got some field glasses and saw that they wore German uniforms. We had a fixed line on the area and I remembered yells and screams from that direction in the night. When it was completely light, and after making sure the area was free of any possible troop concentrations, I went down with a party of three men, each with a shovel.

Approaching cautiously, I probed with care under the bodies in case of any booby-trap devices. We were satisfied that they had just fallen in combat—one had a bullet in the head, while on the other there were no visible marks but he was very dead. No theatre or film studio could fake a man to look like that. After the formalities of identity, we quickly dug one big hole and buried them together. It was most eerie grabbing the stiff, cold forms, and as I let go rivulets of cold sweat tumbled from my forehead, soaking the field grey uniforms with dark spots and creating what seemed to me to be a fraternal feeling. I shook myself free of this absurdity, straightened up, saluted and returned to my position on the crest. Whereupon, any qualms I may have had about the two dead men were soon dispelled by the appearance of two Messerschmitts, which blasted the area with machine gun fire. The cheeky sods even gave a farewell wave on their outward run.

We had only been in Tunisia for a few days and our bag of enemy killed or captured was fast increasing, together with quite an assortment of armoured cars, motorbikes and weapons. To gain more information as to enemy whereabouts, a number of reconnaissance and listening patrols were sent out. I went off in the direction of Mateur with Major Cleasby-Thompson. We made no physical contact with the enemy but had a grandstand view of a large build-up of motorised units and troops on foot. My attention was focused to my right rear as a rock was displaced by a wandering Arab at a distance of only about 20 yards. I clutched my recently acquired German Schmeisser automatic, but luckily he had not seen us. You couldn't be too careful, as some of these Arabs would sell their own mothers for a few francs. We spent the best part of the day taking note of enemy activity in the area stretched out in front of us, with Sedjenane and Mateur in the distance and Djebel Abiod in between.

The Battalion had been most active in the hills, open country and hamlets around Mateur, Medjez el Bab and

Sidi Nsir, and it was to these areas that I found myself going on a volunteer burial party for men known to be lost or killed in action. Our party of six, including Padre Robert Talbot-Watkins, a French officer, a Senegalese scout and an interpreter made ready. Leaving early in the morning, we travelled light in a four-wheel-drive Italian truck captured early on. The truck was strange to drive at first, as the wheels seemed all over the place. However, we soon got used to it and in no time could turn it around in its own length quite expertly. I still hugged my Schmeisser, for although we were just a burial party we had to be ready for any surprises in these barren foothills.

The rainy season was with us but this particular morning was fine and humid and I could see that we were in for a warm day slogging around the gravel desert and granite-like rocky countryside. On foot, we silently cursed the potholes, dips and crevasses, as an ankle would twist, saved only by the tightness of the lace of the boot. Meanwhile, our Senegalese companion would glide over the never-ending obstacles with the ease of a mountain goat. The French officer appeared to fare just as well in his nifty uniform, complete with flowing cape and peaked cap with white crown. For any dead or wounded Paras, the Arabs could be the biggest menace, as some would think nothing of stripping a corpse of its clothing and then just leaving it. If a ring would not come off with ease, the finger might be severed to achieve their greedy end. At times it was reported that wounded of both sides were mutilated by these scum.

The sun was hazy but getting very warm now, and it was only 08.00. Suddenly, a distant shot rang out and I stopped in my tracks, gripping the Schmeisser more firmly and looking in the direction of the shot. That

Senegalese sure could move. He was 150 yards away, with the French officer close on his heels, and had fired his rifle at something 200 yards farther on. I noticed the flurry of an Arab robe flitting from side to side and then disappearing behind a large boulder. Yet another shot rang out, echoing around the hills as the bullet splattered the boulder. The French officer sprinted after the Arab, gesticulating like billy-o upon reaching him. We increased our pace, the Padre doing his utmost to keep up with us. Close by was the cause of the commotion—one of our dead men. Apparently, the Senegalese had seen the Arab bending over the body and had fired a warning shot over his head. The Arab told the officer that he was only looking to see if the British soldier was dead, but I don't think they believed him somehow and sent him packing hell for leather over the distant hill. We set about digging a grave, and after all the preliminary matters had been seen to the Padre said a few prayers. I did not know the young man.

Putting dog tag, papers and other personal items into a bag the Padre carried, we then set off on another search. We covered miles of this god-forsaken country, the Senegalese seeking out friendly Arabs, though questioning them firmly. Arabs seemed to appear from nowhere and I was glad that this particular lot were pro-British. To within a few yards, they directed us to three points where lay the bodies of more of our men. We carried out our burial duties, then, posting a sentry, had a 20-minute breather. It was just after midday. I wished we had not stopped really. I watched as the Senegalese wolfed at some bread and disgusting looking meat pulled from his dirty baggy trousers and I well and truly heaved. It was a relief to set off again, tramping the same type of terrain for another three hours, with the occasional dirt road, its soft cushion-like surface so welcome after the flint and stony drag.

We came upon two more Paras, one lying by a large rock, a jagged cut with dried blood right across his temple. The other, just a few yards away, looking a bloated blue-green. I had seen dead soldiers before, usually just after being killed, but this retrieving of private papers and dog-tags from dead men was not in my book of training and I was lost for a moment, wondering if I was alone in this nightmare. The Padre broke the silence by enquiring in a most serene voice, 'Now, who have we here?' We buried them side-by-side, then found some suitable material for makeshift crosses and slipped their helmets on top. As we made off for base in the gathering dusk I looked back at that black uninviting landscape and called out softly, 'Thanks chaps!'

Things were beginning to hot up now and we found ourselves taking part in some large-scale skirmishes with an enemy who was not going to take it all lying down. We got wind of enemy transport and tank formation in the Sidi Nsir area, which took in a hill known as Sugar Loaf or Gue Hill, and this became our next objective. The Battalion set off almost as if on a training exercise back in England. Little did we know of the disaster that lay ahead for some of us. After a rough ride in transport of all types—Army issue, captured or commandeered— we reached as near as possible to this nasty rock-covered hill. It was while we worked our way around its base that things went haywire.

At about midnight, Captain Pat Geary and some of his sappers had passed by with their load of gear and

Hawkins anti-tank mines strapped to their backs. Then, amid the enemy mortar *stonk* and automatic fire, there suddenly erupted one almighty explosion when the whole party of two-dozen Royal Engineers, including three officers, was blown up by one of the primed Hawkins mines, which in turn detonated the remainder that were being carried. This was a terrible blow for everyone. The sappers did a good job with us and they had such a heavy toll of casualties here at Gue Hill.

I was with Sergeant Dick Whittingham's three-inch mortar gun, of which I had the cumbersome tripod. It was not so much the weight but the awkward shape of the thing that bothered me. The help of the Senegalese troops was most welcome, especially with the conveyance of mortar bombs and the like. Amid the barrage and crackle of small arms fire, I stopped to beckon on the rest of the mortar team as our men swarmed up the hill's almost vertical approach. Panzer Grenadiers and Italian Bersaglieri were holding the top, but were soon dislodged by our men from 'S' and 'R' Companies.

Fortunately, although Italian tanks had been reported in the area, only three were sighted and these were ordered to surrender by Colonel Hill. I was just taking up position with the mortar when the C.O. went round firing his pistol into the open side-slots of the tanks and calling for the crews to come out. On reaching the third tank, shots were fired back and he fell, clutching his chest, followed by his adjutant Captain Miles Whitelock, who was hit in the face. Amid the general din of battle, I was too busy trying to get dug into the rocky soil to make out exactly what had happened but soon learned that the C.O. had been severely wounded and Major Pearson was now to take over the command. It was a great blow to me at this time to hear of the death of my old friend Stanley Wandless.

Despite our losses, we were giving the enemy a hiding and it was good to see the results, even though they often made a disgusting sight. In the vicinity of Mateur, we heard that enemy troops and armour were building up around a place that would come to be known as 'Coxen's Farm' after its occupation by a group of men led by Captain Vic Coxen. On the way to the farm, I passed some knocked-out Italian light tanks, one of which had suffered a direct hit on the driver's compartment. The signs of the driver's last few seconds of agony were plain to see: hands grasped at the chest, head thrown back, mouth open, and eyes too. I went on by another tank but didn't look. When I reached the farm I was horrified by a different sight: an enormous brute of a pig munching away at a dead German soldier. It seemed the pig had somehow come across the wine at the farm, got filthy drunk and was eating everything. Such scenes became horribly familiar but my stomach gradually grew accustomed to them.

At a position we called 'The Ridge', not far from Coxen's Farm, the 1st Battalion was surrounded but never gave an inch. We were being infiltrated at night and put a stop to that by means of firing on a fixed line or by going out to meet the enemy and clobbering him. One day, we had a bit of a shock at the Ridge when eight RAF Bristol Blenheim IV light bombers were shot down by Me 109s. The bombers had been on a mission and were hill-hopping, no doubt hoping to return to base undetected, but their slower speed made them easy targets for the Messerschmitts. Meanwhile, at around

8,000 feet, a squadron of Spitfires was taking evasive action. Maybe this had been a fighter escort for the bombers and was returning to base with ammunition spent. One Blenheim roared but ten feet above my head and I thought I'd had it. It came down 500 yards away, bursting into flames with a loud explosion. We galloped over to the scene, but nothing could be done. I saw another crash three miles away on the Mateur plain. The rest were scattered wrecks over a wide area.

On Christmas Day, 1942, I watched the rainfall as I tried to make myself a little more comfortable in my slit trench. Rain trickled down my neck, my hands were wet and cold, and if I had had a cigarette I would have enjoyed it. My feet had been constantly wet through for god-knows-how-long and I was beginning to feel a teeny bit browned off, when—good news—we were being withdrawn for a rest. Off we went to Souk-el-Khemis, where I thoroughly enjoyed the luxury of a mobile bath unit, delousing and refitting. It was heaven, but we soon returned to the grind once more.

There was now a build-up of American forces, together with the 2nd Lancashire Fusiliers and the 17th/21st Lancers (the 'Death or Glory' boys), whose company we had already had the pleasure of during an earlier assault. One day, after the two Messerchmitts, 'Girt and Daisy', had just made their morning call, 'A' Platoon, along with the mortar team to which I belonged, set off by truck in the direction of Mateur. We had to get across the plain stretched out in front of us to a small area of scattered French dwellings about three miles away. The enemy held the high ground and we wanted to cross in order to keep them on that side of the plain.

Three trucks took us over. It was rough going but we belted across as fast as possible, dodging and weaving to miss oncoming shells and bullets. I hung on to the bar above the truck's driving compartment for dear life and must have been airborne the whole way. The trip was erratic, and for a long while the other side of the plain didn't appear to get any nearer. The three trucks were spread well out and zigzagging to avoid the exploding shells, until at last we were approaching the far side and the shelling became more spasmodic. Our truck came to an abrupt halt alongside some inquisitive Arabs. 'Right', said Sergeant Adcock, 'Over there, get dug in, don't drink any tap water unless it's been sterilized, and keep your eyes peeled for Jerry'. It was a dead and alive place—a sort of semi-front-line position, with the inhabitants still wandering around while we dug holes in their front gardens. And they were none too hospitable either. There was not much likelihood of a properly cooked meal, so we had some tins of food distributed and made do with that.

Just over the road from our mortar position was the edge of the plain, where it began to rise and link up with the hills. To the left, 150 yards away, was a cacti copse and a previous reconnaissance had told us that there was only one way in and out of this. Overnight, Jerry had taken over the copse, maybe to observe our movements, but a vigilant Para saw them and my gun put down a box barrage while a section of men followed up for the kill. The action was short-lived. After a few bombs had been planted and small arms fire spat into the copse, a white flag appeared. These Germans realized that there was no other way as we had them hemmed in. Four were killed and we took six prisoners.

After Christmas the 1st Parachute Brigade was moved out of the line to a place called Boufarik, just outside Algiers. The time spent here would include the minimum of parades, with just a little physical training and the occasional route march to keep us in trim. The billets we were given couldn't have been better, being on the top of wine vats. On arrival we were directed down avenues of orange trees—acres and acres of big, beautiful oranges, just waiting to be picked. I thought I'd like to sample one or two of these once we had settled in, except the French farmer had Arab guards posted with rifles and they didn't look easy to pinch. Fortunately, it didn't matter because we would be given all we could consume.

We stopped at an outbuilding where men from the base were frantically filling palliasses with straw for us. They had heard of our coming but had not got them ready prior to our arrival, so were receiving a hell of a lot of barracking: 'Why are we waiting?' 'Get some in!' 'Take yer bleedin' finger out mate!' I soon had a luxurious palliasse under one arm, my kit bag under the other. I was directed to a long, low, white-painted building, clean and spacious inside, and, above all, dry. Like marauding bands, at a glance Paras would sort out their own spot to bed down and it would be staked out by a kit bag flying through the air to land before anyone else's. I heaved mine with great gusto, while from all around came a clatter of rifle butts and the sound of brass fittings as webbing fell unceremoniously to the deck. What bliss to have one's own body back again after wearing all that paraphernalia for so long!

Liberty trucks were laid on for a visit to Algiers and, along with most of the lads, I could not miss out on the opportunity. After combat conditions it made such a change to see terraced boulevards, a main street of modern buildings, and pleasant parks where French and Arab now intermingled with American and English servicemen taking leisurely walks. The houses on the outskirts, with their bright red roof-tops and barred or shuttered windows, nestled snugly on hillsides among trees and shrubs. It all looked slightly English.

I was walking with my friend Phil and we found ourselves nearing the Arab quarters as an uncouth-looking fellow passed by on a small donkey, giving off an atrocious smell of garlic. The area began to feel sinister and forbidding, so we made a quick about-turn and headed back to the town centre. On the way, we came upon some of those well-known establishments catering for 'horizontal refreshment' where some of our men liked to let off steam. We went into one—naturally, just for a drink. It had the appearance of a smart hotel, with its spotless frontage and glass doors, but inside the aroma of cheap French perfume knocked you for six and the lights were dazzling. Lush young ladies were flimsily dressed and left little to the imagination. We ordered beer, which was four times the price it was outside. It was ghastly, so we switched to wine, which wasn't quite so bad. But the place was getting warm and the air overpowering with cigar smoke, perfume and body odour, so we left and instead found somewhere to eat. A nosh of eggs, steak (so called) and chips went down well but was rather spoilt by the smell of garlic throughout the whole place. An Arab with the worst manners I had ever seen sat at a table supping away at his soup in a way that I'm sure all Algiers could hear. 'Jildi with that soup mate', I said, and with a broad grin he launched into Arabic as if he'd never stop. He must have thought he'd made a friend for life and edged nearer. He was still grinning when we left him to his smelly soup.

On another visit to Algiers with Phil and Jock, we teamed up with two American parachutists and, like old hands, went around the town painting it thoroughly red until night was suddenly upon us. We had all won the war and could not care less for anyone when a vehicle pulled up and I noticed a familiar sight: highly polished British Army boots, razor creases in trousers, gaiters, belt, gun holsters scrubbed white and peaked caps pulled down over the eyes. I could have been back in London but instead this was my first run-in with Redcaps in Africa. As it was, they were quite amiable. The sergeant said, 'You won't get back to Boufarik tonight', and the lance corporal added, 'Nasty place, this, at night, especially after a few noggins.' Unaware that it was for our own safety, we were then locked up in the Algiers civilian nick for the night. It was uncomfortable trying to sleep on a slanting stone slab. I awoke with two Arabs on one side, a French soldier on the other, and Jock, Phil and the two Yanks on the far side of him. I was so glad to get out of that place. It must have been a thousand years old.

Chapter Six
Red Devils

Back in Tunisia the Germans were making a concentrated effort to shift the British and American forces from the Bouarada area, and it was to there that we were now sent. We travelled by boat from Algiers to Bone, and from Bone to Bouarada in trucks. The latter stage was a dark, wet and dismal journey, though the strong wind and heavy rain provided good cover for any noise we made transporting our men and supplies. In Bouarada the enemy was trying to bottle us up in a pincer movement, thrusting from a place called Goubellat, 12 miles to the north, from Sloughia, 14 miles to the north-west, and from El Aroussa, 10 miles to the west. They were also pushing hard at Kasserine, 110 miles to the south, where the Americans were.

Fifteen miles south-east of Bouarada is Pont-du-Fahs, and between the two towns is a hill called Djebel Mansour, the commanding height to the Pont-du-Fahs/Tunis road. It is 2,000 feet above sea level, five miles around the base, and has an easiest climbing angle of 45 degrees. Also known by us as Hill 648, it was occupied by crack German Africa Corps and Alpine troops and it was our job to take it at all costs. I thought this would be a tough nut to crack but the men were determined to win through and shift the enemy once and for all. We checked our arms and ammunition and collected 48 hours' rations.

In the dim light of the early morning I saw Major Pearson marshalling men to their given starting-off points, using his old pipe as a map pointer. Peter Stainforth, an officer with the Royal Engineers, passed with some of his men, loaded and ready for their part, and some of 'T' Company glided by like ghosts, guided by Major Conron, their gear letting off a slight tinkling sound as brass buckles clipped other items. I was local defence and bomb carrier on Sergeant Adcock's three-inch mortar gun. 'We are moving in five minutes', he quietly informed us.

We started off, and it was quite a long way over rough uneven ground before we halted at the base of an ugly, massive-looking hill. The usual advance-bombardment that preceded most attacks was not forthcoming on this occasion, as we wanted to maintain the element of surprise. This time, Jerry would be the first to rock the boat. As we waited at the base of the hill the sky now and again became bright with German night-lights, which when fired heavenward made the whole area quite luminous. Everyone froze until they fell to earth and safety returned once more in the form of semi-darkness. In this waiting game I found my thoughts straying back to England. What I could do to a couple of pints of English beer.

It was not until four o'clock the next morning that we ventured carefully forward through the undergrowth. Up went more German night-lights—two, then two more, then more still. The place was illuminated like daylight. They must have got wind of us, or smelt us. We could determine the nationality of a soldier at fifty feet if the wind was favourable, so probably they could do the same. From the top of the hill two machine guns began firing, then more joined in as though the place were alive with them, and they slashed and ripped mercilessly at the bracken, slicing the branches of trees as if an invisible sharp knife had done the job. A bullet went through my trouser leg, grazing my thigh, but I didn't think too much of it as I was still mobile. German mortars started hitting the approach slope and yells of pain here and there told me to take more care. The whine overhead was also a warning that enemy artillery was joining in. As things hotted up, with the occasional tracer bullet mixed in with the machine gun fire, I could almost feel the hot lead piercing my limbs and was certain I would not get away with it this time.

Farther back, things had gone wrong with our usually stalwart mules (the amazing animals that carried our heavy gear where men could not set foot). They didn't appreciate the sudden shelling and bolted, out of control. Major Cleasby-Thompson managed to round some of them up with the help of a French officer, Major Prioleau, and then all hell seemed to be let loose, our men yelling 'Who-oooh-Mohamed!' as 'R' and 'T' Companies went in with their bayonets. Unfortunately, 'S' Company missed their correct route—the tapes laid to assist their ascent had been damaged or cut by enemy activity—and at the count we were to find that they had suffered extremely heavy casualties.

The barrage we were up against was intense and a ricocheting bullet or shell splinter often did as much damage, or more, than a straightforward burst of fire. We could occasionally be lucky—at one time an artillery shell failed to explode on impact with the ground and went on merrily ricocheting three times before coming to rest with a dull *phlop*. But the bombardment was unrelenting and we really had our work cut out here. There were agonizing shrieks of pain right and left of me as I passed men, unrecognizable, soaked in blood, being tended by our splendid medics—those unsung, unarmed heroes! Sam Coster and Frankie Thompson had reached the summit and searched out and dealt with the enemy with no ceremony whatsoever. As Sam told me afterwards, Frankie was lunging and tossing men with his bayonet as though they were sacks of straw. Frankie was a big chap, usually very friendly and quietly spoken, but in action a different man. His Guards and para-commando training served us well on that day.

It was daylight by the time I reached the top, after hours of continuous mortar and machine gun fire. Every inch of ground had been ferociously fought for, as the Germans did not give up without giving as good as they were dealt. Amid all the turmoil and dead and wounded of both sides, the curtain of fire had lifted and there was not a sound. Looking around the hilltop, only a few of our men could be seen moving among the twisted forms. Our 'R', 'T' and 'S' Companies had suffered very heavy casualties. More than half of the Battalion's officers had been killed or wounded.

I came across our Medical Officer Doc Haggie, who said the situation was in hand but that we had few men left to hold the hill, and the enemy was sure to counterattack. He ordered me to help in getting the wounded from the forward positions to a place where they could get proper treatment, back in the direction of Bouarada. Setting about the job of collecting the wounded was something sickening. As I gazed upon the scene of our once able and live comrades, now quite still or with torn limbs, I wondered whether there was any such thing as civilisation. I bit hard on my lip and went about my task with grim determination.

Looking around for someone to help, I noticed a lad who was in the same troop as me early in 1941. 'Hello

Taffy! And what have you been up to? Like a lift?' 'Cheers, Lofty, it's nice to see someone alive', he said, wearily. He was in a sitting position and had apparently been hit by no fewer than five bullets. They were all clean flesh wounds—in the calf, thigh, forearm, and one through the apex of the penis—and all rather uncomfortable, but no broken bones. He was pretty well saturated with blood, but cheerful. 'Let's try a fireman's carry', I suggested. He'd had a shot of morphine, so I didn't think he would feel much. 'Anything to get away from here', he said.

At that point, Jerry started up again with artillery and mortars, then a few snipers, and, to make it really interesting, some Stuka dive-bombers joined in the chorus. 'Let's get going before it gets too hot. I've got to get you on my back', I said. I managed to get him over my shoulder without causing too much pain and we started the long trek through wooded country, ravines and open waste. I found it impossible to carry him downhill because the gradient was too great, so we sat awhile and I thought about it while drawing heavily on a cigarette and assisting Taffy with his. I asked if he could ease himself down with his hands while I guided him by the ankles, and he said he'd give it a go. It was a ticklish and tender job, but for two hours we struggled on. I was sweating like two pigs.

We reached the bottom of the hill and looked back. I could see the relief in Taffy's face at the thought of getting away from that place, but we were not clear yet and a sniper had spotted us. I grabbed Taffy again and got moving, bullets striking dangerously near. Trudging on, sometimes hiding from view by crawling with him on my back, we reached more open country and took another breather. Not for long, though, as shellfire warned us to move on again. We had been going for two hours but had only covered one-and-a-half miles. By the time we finally arrived at the first aid post we must have travelled a six-mile route all told. I saw Taffy put into a jeep with other wounded and that was the last I saw or heard of him. I didn't hang about for long. Every shell told me to get cracking back to Djebel Mansour to the remains of my Battalion.

After arriving back at the mountain, we had a fairly quiet night except for the coming and going of patrols, but the following day dawned with fresh trouble. Enemy 20mm quick-firing cannon and 105mm mortars were causing us great discomfort. Our own three-inch mortars, with the close support (too close sometimes) of our 25-pounders, were reciprocating. It was the 4th of February.

I joined a section comprising men from 'T' and 'S' Companies. They were mostly newcomers. I wondered what had become of all the friends I had not seen since the attack started. One of the lads told me that Major Conron had been killed, and Captain Mellor too. I felt so alone—no disrespect to the reinforcements, but the cream of our men were fast disappearing in the foothills of Tunisia.

Jerry was counterattacking in earnest now and slinging everything at us in the way of explosives, with batches of Stuka dive-bombers joining in at two-hour intervals and making things even more deafening. The muck was falling heavily and a splinter from a nearby bursting mortar bomb slashed a vein in my right hand, while another pranged my helmet. One man had a horrible gash in his left arm, but thankfully no bone was broken and a quick tourniquet and field dressing did the trick. We hung on desperately until late afternoon, when, due to heavy casualties and lack of ammunition, we were ordered to withdraw to Bouarada.

Nipping over rocks and creeping through bracken and bush under a hail of bullets and screaming shells, I became cut off from the party of men I'd been attached to. I was making good progress and, stopping for a breather, dropped into a small depression in the ground. Suddenly, a lone German pounced on me from the rear. I realised what was happening instantly when I saw the field-grey cuff of his uniform. My Schmeisser, which was out of ammunition, was slung bandoleer-fashion over my shoulder but I had an American .45 automatic Colt at the ready in my right hand. I went down on one knee, summoned up the unarmed combat I had been taught, grabbed him by the scruff of the neck and heaved him with all my force over my head. It was my turn now and I was not so gentle. As he rolled on to his back, I sprang and landed my 14-stone weight feet-first on his chest. Grabbing the Colt, which I had released to dangle on its lanyard, I started to squeeze the trigger, shouting, 'You butcher bastard' to his 'No, no, comrade, no, no, no'. I pulled the trigger, but it was empty. I grabbed his rifle, checked that it was loaded and ordered him to his feet. 'Danke, danke', he kept saying, hugging his chest as we moved off, and gibbering 'Nicht verstehen'—I don't understand.

Arriving back in Bouarada, after the formality of delivering my prisoner into custody, I rejoined the rest of the Battalion. We were in great need of a rest and a refit and were all sent by truck to a place called Teboursouk, some 60 miles off, while Bouarada was handed over, with thanks, to the Americans.

We were very soon back with the Brigade, this time in the Djebel Abiod area. Trouble was brewing between Tamera, the 'Happy Valley', and Nefza, just a little south of a hill we called the 'Pimple', with the River Oued el Madene running a short distance away. We were ceaselessly attacked by enemy troops flown in fresh from Sicily and Italy, and dive-bombers and fighters paid regular visits. Movement in daytime was tricky to say the least. The Brigade's manpower was well down and the enemy usually outnumbered us three to one. 'Death Ridge', as my 1st Para position in Happy Valley was known, also developed the name 'Shell Shock Ridge'. I tried closing my eyes at any given explosion. It was a terrible feeling, like waiting to be massacred.

The Germans started to mount an attack. It was daylight and I could see motorised enemy units being dropped off at points as near as they dared to our positions—three or four miles off in the direction of Sedjenane. They spread out in extended order and started towards us. We were told to hold our fire until the last minute, so the whole 1st Battalion lay very quiet and still. Enemy mortars saturated the area. I felt the draught of an exploding shell, which deafened my left ear and left it ringing, and at the same time propelled me to the bottom of my trench, making me even wetter than I already was. My wristwatch was submerged in water but when I hoisted myself up to ground level again it was still going. It must be waterproof, I thought.

Now the mortar barrage had lifted, and I could hear the slice of Solothurn machine gun fire as it severed the undergrowth, the enemy getting nearer all the time— sixty yards; fifty yards; forty yards. I peeked gingerly over the edge of my hole in the ground. Thirty yards;

twenty yards; then, above the din, the order was bellowed: 'Fire! Fire! Fire! Advance! Advance!' As we went out to meet them, the Battalion flung everything at the enemy that it could—Tommy guns, Bren guns, Sten guns, captured Solothurns and Schmeissers, grenades (English, German and Italian)—coupled with the cry of 'Who-oooh-Mohamed!' Gripping my rifle, I advanced through the murderous fire, the haze of smoke and the acrid smell of explosive. Every available man was in on this one, even the cooks. Before long the tables had turned in our favour. With two dead Paras laying to my left, I hopped over a dead German and came upon a wounded one a little to my right. He was contemplating using a Luger pistol but I booted it from his hand and clomped him in the face with the butt of my rifle. The whole episode was soon over, with the enemy beating a hasty retreat and leaving a bag of captured, clean-shaven German parachutists, flown in direct from Germany to deal with us. What a shock for them!

Similar successes were reported from our other two battalions, as the whole of the 1st Parachute Brigade was involved in this clash, with 2 Para slightly to our right in Cork Wood and 3 Para in the woods on the other side of Tamera. Further British troops who were of great assistance to us there were the gallant lads of the 2nd/5th Leicesters, the Sherwood Foresters and the Yorks and Lancs. After a while, we were taken out of the front line once again and this time sent to Tabarka, a coastal town 24 miles away, for refitting and a rest, though the area was under shellfire and frequent air-attack, so it was not altogether restful. Once again it was a short respite and in no time we were back in Happy Valley.

There was to be a coordinated attack by our Brigade Group upon units of Panzer Grenadiers, German parachutists and Italian Bersagliere on a ridge to the left of the main road, between the Pimple and another hill we named 'Bowler Hat'. The operation entailed the crossing of the River Oued el Madene. It was a night attack and an intense artillery barrage would be put down. While we pushed on with 2 Para, and 3 Para brought up the rear, the British 139th Brigade attacked on our right. In time the Pimple was retaken and our Brigade proceeded to press home the final assault amidst devastating artillery and mortar fire from both sides. Tragically, we found that we had gone a little too fast for our 25-pounders to increase their range quickly enough and we suffered heavy casualties from our own fire. At daylight, I passed Jock Pearson, crouched by a rock bellowing into a field radio and none too pleased with the person on the other end. 'What do you think you're doing?' he roared, 'you're killing all my bwoody men'. (He never could pronounce his 'L's or 'R's and always referred to Rommel as 'Wommel'.)

Cleaning up the area, 1st Para took up positions while 3 Para pushed on. Meanwhile, 2 Para had a temporary setback with some Panzer Grenadiers, but won through in the end. Then, after the shock of our coordinated attack, the enemy counterattacked, laying on a hell of a barrage. But everything seemed to be in our favour now—even the weather was kinder—and we must have advanced about eight miles under a curtain of continuous fire, until both Italians and Germans were ready to give in and were running to be captured.

In April the First Army built up substantial supplies of equipment and men, and very soon we started pushing again, this time with good air cover. We were approaching Sedjenane, the scene of heavy fighting and tank battles, and for three days the enemy gave us hell with low-level machine-gunning and delayed-action bombing. Along the way, I came across numerous knocked-out enemy tanks. Remembering Gue Hill, where our C.O. had been shot by an occupant of a tank, I approached the first with the greatest caution. I saw, though, that it had been efficiently put out of action by a direct hit on the driver's compartment. A devastating ugly hole, some 18 inches in diameter, had been torn and revealed the grotesque sight of the driver with his guts hanging out. The poor chap could not have known much.

Messerschmitts buzzed the area, spraying the ground spasmodically and causing those nearest to drop quickly into convenient holes. We pushed on at a steady pace, past demolished guns and supply dumps, the air stinking with appalling butchery. I glanced instinctively towards a shell-burst 50 yards away and as I watched its jet-black smoke belch skyward my gaze was transfixed by something odd on the ground. I wondered if it could be human. Drawing nearer, I saw that it was the roasted body of a man in the sitting position. He must have been driving a scout car or light vehicle as there were small pieces of charred twisted metal spread 50 feet around, with dismembered arms and legs and torn, blood-soaked uniforms littering the black scorched soil. The aroma was diabolical. Someone accidentally brushed the sitting form on passing and the body simply disintegrated with a sickly sound.

There were now knocked-out Italian Carro Armato tanks everywhere. Whatever had hit them had made a good job, with direct hits either on the drivers' compartments or the caterpillar wheel-tracks. I also counted four wrecked Autoblinda 40 armoured cars. As we worked our way through, cleaning out any pockets of resistance, someone shouted 'Focke-Wulfs' and I spotted three nosing in for an attack upon our transport along the Sedjenane road. I felt fairly safe from air attack myself, as my section was about 150 yards from the road and the enemy aircraft were only interested in the road transport. Of the six trucks, spread well out within my sight, not one got hit, but then a pair of Me 109s followed up with machine-gunning, joined by enemy rocket mortars situated behind a hill—'sobbing sisters' we called them, due to the screaming sound they made. The attack lasted some minutes. After many explosions and *crumps*, as mortar shells burst too near for comfort, the enemy planes slunk off, sent on their way by our light mobile ack-ack. Once again all was quiet.

Men began moving from places of safety to check on casualties and inspect possible damage. Miraculously, no one had been hurt, though one vehicle was smoking, so another was hailed and hands worked feverishly to transfer gear from the crippled vehicle into it. Momentarily relieved at the lack of anything more serious, I returned my attention to one of those Italian armoured cars, its metal scorched and twisted as though it were just made of tin, its occupants still in combat positions but quite dead. The smell of burnt flesh floated in my direction and I quickened my pace to get clear of it. Plodding on in these awful humid and dusty conditions, I think I felt almost immune to weariness and the shocking sights of war. Nothing seemed able to stop us now.

The 1st Parachute Brigade Group was not destined to take part in the final push to Tunis. Our role in the campaign had come to an end and we were withdrawn from the line, so ending five months' hard slog. Originally trained as shock troops, in Tunisia after the initial parachute assaults we had served as plain infantry, but that's just the way the wind blew for us. Medals were plentiful and all ranks had earned them: eight Distinguished Service Orders, fifteen Military Crosses, nine Distinguished Conduct Medals, twenty-two Military Medals, three Croix de Guerre, and one Legion d'Honneur. In their own way, even our German adversaries had recognised the Brigade's fighting ability by naming us the 'Rote Teufel', or 'Red Devils'. For those who were there, though, the price of success was unspeakably high. We had lost more than 1,700 men killed, wounded or missing.

Chapter Seven
Sicily

From Tunisia we were transported back to Algeria, where we found a new temporary home in and around an Arab hamlet called Matemore on the fringe of the great Plain of Mascara, some 60 miles from Oran. The American Air Force had already put in an appearance with their Dakota aircraft, letting us know that something new was afoot, and it turned out that for the next two months we would be training hard for a drop into Sicily. It was hoped that if Sicily could be taken it might prompt an Italian surrender.

A large proportion of my Battalion, including myself, now went down with dysentery, which was not really surprising, given the abundance of grapefruit, tangerine, orange and passion fruit, together with the vast plague of flies. No sooner had you swiped a couple from your arm or neck than two more would take their place. The toilets, situated on the side of a hill, were kept busy day and night, with men running up the incline feverishly undoing their trousers ready for action. The toilet was crude, though efficient. The seat, straddling a deep pit, was a six-foot pole and we had to be careful of splinters. The hole was surrounded by a canvas screen for a little privacy but was open to the heavens. One could hear the constant slapping of buttocks, each slap registering the end of yet another infernal fly.

We managed to get in some training jumps and, during one, I was worried to find myself being propelled upwards, rather than falling to earth, due to the fact that the warm under-current was arrested inside the canopy. I didn't want to finish up in Casablanca, so grabbed the lift webb—one of the 28 webbing lines connected to the parachute—and pulled hard, trying to spill the air. Nothing happened. I was still going steadily up, with hot air encircling me and making it uncomfortable to breathe. I tried to oscillate by kicking both legs from side to side and slowly managed to gather some momentum. Yanking again on the lift webb, gradually the air spilled and I started to descend, continuing to spill air until I was safely down. It was a fortunate ending to another unsupervised lesson in parachuting.

Between exercises, we acclimatized our reinforcements to the use of enemy weapons, including the Schmeisser automatic, which we found superior to our own Sten gun. A Sten was likely to jam or accidentally go off upon receiving a sharp tap, so was gladly swapped for a Schmeisser, which used the same calibre ammunition. We were also eager to pass on first-hand knowledge and skills in unarmed combat, learned by us the hard way, along with the ethics of modern warfare. One lad looked bewildered and rather aghast at being told that when the enemy is grounded, if nothing else, you put the boot in. A Welshman standing next to me couldn't have put it better when he said softly, 'Boyo, you've to bend the rules of human decency a bit, otherwise you won't get anywhere with this lot out here, you see?' I think our friend was convinced.

During this period of training we received a lightning visit from US General Dwight Eisenhower, who had been Allied Commander-in-Chief of the invasion of North Africa and now had the job of organizing the invasion of Sicily. General Eisenhower and his entourage were only with us for half an hour at the most, during which someone heard him make a comment about being impressed with our khaki drill shorts. I was not so keen myself as they were a little too thin for comfort when the temperature dropped.

There were three bridges to take in Sicily: Ponte Grande at Syracuse, Ponte dei Malati over the River Leonardo, and the most northerly, which was allotted to the 1st Parachute Brigade Group, Primosole Bridge over the River Simeto, south of Catania. Under Brigade Commander Brigadier Gerald Lathbury, with Colonels Pearson, Frost and Yeldman in command of our 1st, 2nd and 3rd Battalions, respectively, the plan to capture Primosole Bridge was codenamed 'Operation Fustian'. We were to prevent it being destroyed until our Army had pushed through and passed over it, and so on to Catania. It was estimated that this could save eight days' fighting and many lives. Our password was to be 'Desert Rats', with the reply 'Kill Italians'.

On the 12th of July I was at an airstrip talking with the American pilots as we prepared for the hop. Zero hour was not far off when a truck arrived with some tea and eats, and soon lines of C47 and C53 Dakotas were humming with the movement of men boarding, containers being adjusted and ground staff going about the job of refuelling. At 20.00 we climbed into our aircraft. As the plane took off, Chunky said, 'Well, this is it—our second operation'. I tried to act normally but could feel the sweat running down my cheek.

After two hours we passed over Malta—one more hour to go before the drop. Private Irons seemed at ease. Private Pearce was amused by something he was reading in a coloured comic. Western looked as if he were going home from work on a bus. Chunky and I were both tense. To avoid detection of our approach, the aircraft was 'wave-hopping' at only fifty feet, before climbing gradually as we approached land. I looked out of the doorway and could see huge fires burning along the Sicilian coastline from Syracuse to Catania. Passing over British naval ships and merchantmen, we found that ship-to-air recognition was not what it should have been and were subjected to ack-ack fire from those very ships. Then, to make our welcome even more memorable the enemy joined in. Searchlights fanned the sky to find us. Flak and machine gun fire streamed skyward as if it would never cease.

We drew nearer to our objective and at 1,000 feet I could see flak and tracer zipping past under the wing of the aircraft. For 30 minutes we dodged everything they threw at us, but it was a tense half hour as we were helpless to do anything. Suddenly, we were given the order to 'hook up'. I did so and waited. As the engines cut back on the approach to our drop zone, we descended to around 600 feet, with all sorts of rubbish whizzing by and the plane pitching and tossing like a toy in a vast vacuum. Then there came a terrific explosion as our tail was hit. The order: 'Jump man—jump!' screamed in my ears and I tumbled through the doorway into the void below.

My parachute opened and I saw the dots of my pals as they drifted dimly around me. Searchlights were turned on and found us no matter how much we twisted and turned to seek the comfort of the darkness. Flak burst very near and the enemy opened up with machine gun fire. A tracer bullet clipped one of the rigging lines to my parachute, which collapsed lazily over my shoulder as I landed very heavily on a road. I found cover in a gaping ditch and began to get my bearings.

Military-wise, you could say that I was lucky, provided I managed to reach the bridge, because less than a third of our Brigade had actually made it to the drop zones. Owing to the American pilots' limited experience of enemy action and the flak bursting among them, some had headed back to base in North Africa, while some had lost their way and some had finished up in the sea. A number of our men were dropped off course as far as Catania and even as far away as Italy. Captain Dicky Dover of the 2nd Para Battalion dropped on Mount Etna—not a very nice place to be when it erupts, which is fairly frequently. In Sergeant Beech's aircraft was C.O. Jock Pearson, who noticed the plane turning for home and had pulled his revolver on the pilot, firmly telling him to get back on course.

On the ground, about 300 yards to my left, was the main coastal road to the town of Catania and enemy traffic was in tremendous confusion. To my rear I could hear Italian voices, and about 100 yards to my right Germans rapping out orders. Then, down the road came a 15-strong German patrol. They could have been parachutists, judging by their dress and headgear. Fortunately, I was not alone and when they were just a few yards off we opened up on them. There were some grunts, groans and sickly yelps, then silence. We slipped on in the direction of the bridge, around which our men were by now silently killing, harassing and panicking the German and Italian defenders. My section found it hard to join up with them because of the large number of irrigation ditches and the boggy surrounding ground, which made progress very slow. We hit a track leading to the main road but as our feet touched it a volley of German Schmeisser automatic fire came from the west side of the road. We scrambled into a ditch and answered with some enthusiasm.

All night, small battles raged unceasingly and we were pinned down for a long time by mortar fire. This lifted for a while and a passing patrol of ours told us that the bridge had been taken and we should stay put until morning. When daylight broke through, I saw for the first time the vast mountain scenery, at the base of which we had been fighting. High above, to the north of Catania, was the rounded cone of the volcano Etna, while to the west was the plain of Trapani.

It became warm, and then the heat became intense. There had been no firing for some time and I realised that the enemy was no longer with us. Scanning the countryside, I could see burnt-out cars, Italian tanks and ammunition dumps. The smell of burnt bodies and oil filled the air. I was glad to move on. Such was the confusion of our Brigade drop, that come daylight three men from 3 Para discovered they had spent the night fighting alongside men of 1st Para without realising it.

At the bridge it was clear that there had been a fierce battle. The pillboxes had been rushed and dealt with ruthlessly. Here, the Brigade mustered approximately 180 men, but the three-inch mortars and ammunition had not arrived and there was a lack of communication with outside units. Wireless sets had either been incorrectly netted back in Africa, were damaged on landing or just did not arrive. We learned that German parachutists from the 3rd Regiment of the 1st Fallschirmjager Division had dropped simultaneously on our drop zone the previous night, so we must indeed have brushed shoulders when we came upon that 15-man patrol.

Along with Chunky, I now settled down in a ready-made slit trench, a few feet away from the steel work of the southern end of the bridge. Our men were busy consolidating positions, the Royal Engineers were engaged in dismantling explosive charges attached to the bridge, Jerry was lying doggo, and it felt almost like another exercise—but not for long. At about 10.30 two Focke-Wulfs began to attack. Their aerodrome was only a few miles away and it was a smooth process for them—they would take off, machine-gun us, return to base, land and reload, then take off and carry out the same procedure again and again. Thankfully, the British Navy stepped in and warships we could not see shelled the aerodrome so effectively that no more planes took off. We cheered like mad.

The enemy was not giving up and tried a new tactic, using their flak guns as artillery. This went on all day, with intervals only while German troops carried out attacks. Watching flak shells burst at a normal height of ten or twelve thousand feet is reasonably comfortable, but at twelve feet it is a different matter. Ugly black balls of smoke would appear one after the other, accompanied by a coughing sound and the distribution of whirring shrapnel. One lump hit the steel bridge above me and ricocheted dangerously near my head, embedding itself in the back of the slit trench. Then a piece hit me in the side, stinging sharply for a few seconds. It had torn my webb belt and penetrated my trousers, shirt and jumping jacket. On inspection, I saw a small jagged piece sitting in the flesh. It was still warm as I extracted it. Chunky was joking about how lucky I was to be presented with a souvenir, when he was hit in the leg—again nothing much, thankfully. 'They must like you too, mate', I said.

Captain Gammon (the officer who had thought up the Gammon Bomb) belted by with Lance Corporal Osborne close behind. There was a huge *crump* as a load of muck fell around us, and a lump of concrete slithered along the bridge as one of the concrete pillboxes got a pounding. Pat O'Brien asked me the time. 'I don't know,' I said. 'A lump of bloody shrapnel put my watch out of action.' There was quite a clatter going on now. Brigadier Lathbury had been wounded but was still able to conduct operations, while Jock Pearson was busy sorting out the situation on the north end of the bridge. Little wonder things were so warm—the area within an approximately two-mile radius of the bridge was festooned with 88mm and 20mm guns, pillboxes, machine gun pits and also a few coastal guns, and we were engaging with crack German troops, including paratroops. They presented a good target whenever they got too near to the bridge— you could not miss—but word went around that our supply of ammunition was now drastically low. 'Conserve ammunition and fire only when you are absolutely certain of a kill' was the order.

In due course, members of the 1st and 3rd Para Battalions at the northern end of the bridge withdrew to join us at the southern end. The enemy was getting harder to ward off and tanks began to appear. Fortunately, the Royal Engineers had made a good job of dismantling the explosive charges around the bridge, or there would have been an almighty explosion, with all of us going up too. Suddenly, there was a resounding explosion to my rear, followed by another. Jerry had brought up an 88mm gun and put paid to the two concrete pillboxes behind us—one just behind me to the left and the other on the opposite side of the approach road. Between the two were store sheds for mines, shells and small arms ammunition, which went up too. We were using a captured Italian 40mm anti-tank gun, along with our own anti-tank gun. The battle worked up to a terrific climax. The Germans were sending in their best troops in an effort to shift us, their paratroopers probing for weak spots and allowing no respite. Food was in our haversacks but there was no time to get at it—it was fire, fire and keep on firing.

Finally, there was a lull at about 18.30, or soon after, giving us a chance to take stock. Maybe the Germans wanted to regroup. I checked my ammunition and found only four rounds left, plus one in the chamber. At 19.30 we were ordered to withdraw in order to avoid capture, and to go in small groups. We did not then know that the forward elements of our own armour would arrive in three hours, otherwise we would most likely have held on with our bare hands for those 180 vital minutes. Glancing around the area of the bridge we had been defending for the last 12 hours, I searched the tired faces for anyone I knew. 'Come on', shouted Chunky, 'let's git before Jerry comes to!' Pat Dolan joined us.

We made off in a westerly direction towards the Gorna Lunga River. If we could use the river and the road running parallel to it as a guide for a couple of miles, perhaps by then we would be clear of any concentrated enemy attack. We had not much ammunition between us, so to steer clear of the enemy was the best bet. Skirting the drop zone of the previous night, we turned eastward into and along a dried-up ditch that afforded cover. There was the occasional sound of small arms fire, together with the odd shell passing overhead. Breaking cover, we were fired upon from a hilltop about 600 yards to the west, so we dodged in among trees and bushes and the firing ceased.

Coming into the open again to enter an adjoining field, we unexpectedly found ourselves confronted by a group of 50 Italians. I am certain that my heart stopped beating and my blood ran cold. They made no move to challenge us, so we took the initiative and challenged them. They put up their hands. Most were young, and some were beyond the age for soldiering. They carried cases, bundles or holdalls, all ready as if to go away somewhere. No one said anything and it was getting embarrassing. 'I'll try out my Italian', I said to Chunky and Pat, and tried, but to no effect. Then, an Italian officer stepped forward and saluted, saying in good English, 'We are glad you are here and are ready to surrender!' We frankly did not know what to do with 50 prisoners—to take them with us would run the risk of being fired upon by our own troops or Air Force, so we told them to stay put until our forces pushed forward, and they would be looked after then. The officer gladly agreed and they sat down like children at our command. While Chunky covered them, Pat and I collected up their rifles and smashed them over a boulder, hanging on to two neat-looking Beretta pistols. With an assurance that they would be taken care of tomorrow, we backed away, still covering them, until we felt it was safe to turn and carry on.

As darkness fell we came upon a deserted farmhouse but decided not to enter as it was quite near an abandoned flak gun pit. We thought both could be booby-trapped. Pushing on for about five miles, we encountered no one, friend or foe. Unlike mine, Chunky's watch was still going and it was approximately

02.00 by now. We were very tired and hungry. We dozed in an orchard, twenty feet from the edge—each man at the base of a different tree so as to be less conspicuous. At about 03.00 the sound of marching feet on the secondary road only thirty feet away brought us rudely to. A German patrol, ten-strong and heavily armed with Schmeissers and rifles, was passing by. If they spotted us, we'd had it. With all that firepower, and given the situation, I doubt they would have bothered with prisoners. I moulded myself slowly and more deeply into the shadow afforded by the trees. Thankfully, they passed right by. Some time later we heard quite a concentrated amount of German and English automatic and rifle fire, which told us that they must have met up with some of our lads. When it was light enough we drew hard on a cigarette, enjoying it to the full after being without during the night.

Setting off once again, we saw no more of the enemy. Via Lentini, we reached Augusta, some 15 miles from the Primosole Bridge. Finding the town in our hands, it was a great sight to see so many of our own troops and tanks. For the tanks, it must have been difficult negotiating the narrow winding roads in this mountainous country—one slip and it could be goodbye tank down a rocky 400-foot drop. We managed to scrounge a lift in a troop-carrying vehicle of the Royal Army Service Corps heading for Syracuse, the three of us tailboard-hanging the whole way, always ready for a quick exit in case of air attack. I reckon that the Army can thank us for saving that vehicle and the lives of the four RASC men in it, as the driver didn't realise how near to the edge of the mountain road he was when shunting back and forth to negotiate one hairpin bend.

'Hold it you clot', shouted Chunky, and three men never moved so fast as when we leapt off. We put our shoulders to the task and I shouted instructions to the driver who moved slowly forward with just inches to spare.

Reaching Syracuse without mishap on the 17th of July, just four days after dropping into Sicily, we soon set sail, arriving back at Sousse in Tunisia on the 20th. Our 1st Parachute Brigade Group had not only suffered heavily in the North African campaign, but in Sicily too, where we had lost a further 300 men killed, wounded or missing. It was time to rest, refit, regroup and reorganise, and we also got to relax. We watched film shows and visited Tunis; we took it easy while we could. The Brigade was to be held in reserve for the 1st Airborne Division's next action in September—an amphibious landing at Taranto in Italy, where Mussolini had stepped down and Italian and German troops were fast retreating. There were mixed feelings among the men about why airborne forces were to be involved in an amphibious landing at all. In the event, the landing was unopposed and we were not called upon.

In early November we were told that the whole 1st Airborne Division was returning to England and the 1st Parachute Brigade would leave from Algiers at the end of the month. On the 29th of November we shipped out of Algiers on the *S.S. Samaria*, happily heading for Liverpool. On board, as usual, everyone scrambled for what they thought was the best position for the trip home. I just beat Wally Boldock and Albert Osborne to a spot right near the mess table. The form was the same as on the trip out to Africa a little over a year ago, with boat-drill and physical training, films to watch, card games to play and plenty of food if you could eat it.

Now, one particular chap made a popular appearance—Peter, the Battalion's (unofficial) loveable dog. Peter liked water and jumping from planes and was the only parachuting dog on record. At first he was owned by a lad named Topper Brown and rumour had it they had both escaped from Dunkirk in 1940. Peter was a marvel and could do almost anything asked of him, never forgetting a trick. Put a stone on his nose and back away and he'd remain motionless, but at a given command would toss and catch that stone. Water was his god! There had been static tanks eight feet deep at Bulford into which a stone would be thrown. Peter would retrieve it in no time and then sit patiently awaiting another run. When we had set off for North Africa in October the previous year he had been smuggled aboard the *Arundel Castle*, everyone helping in the scheming to get him aboard and keep him fed, exercised and comfortable. He had been left behind in Algeria in the good care of the cooks and rear echelon party while we went on to meet the enemy in Tunisia, where Topper Brown was taken prisoner and sadly never heard of again.

Corporal Jim Nash, the Battalion hairdresser of 'R' Company, then took care of Peter and it was at Matemore in Algeria, during training for the Sicily operation, that Jim took him up for his first jump from an aircraft. A special bag had been made and was fixed to Jim's front, with a hole at the top for Peter's head to protrude. They made a perfect landing, Peter running off as happy as Larry, wagging his tail. After various other escapades, Peter returned to Algiers and was smuggled aboard the *Samaria*, where he was having a great time until the locker door of his hiding place was accidentally left unsecured during one of our boat-drill procedures and he ventured out on his own. He was found wandering below by the Ship's Officer who ordered him to be put over the side. We were just two days out from Liverpool. The men were furious and it was just as well that the officer responsible could not be found, as a roving band of justice-seeking Paras could not have been expected to be lenient. As far as Peter was concerned, he had such enthusiasm for water that maybe it was fitting to end up in a sea grave, but we felt his loss. I don't mind admitting that we fighting men had a soft side, even after all we'd seen and done, perhaps especially after all we'd seen and done. I wrote Peter a poem entitled 'Epitaph to a Friend', its last verse as follows:

> Peter made us happy and carefree,
> He had no military apparel,
> He made just two jumps; his grave is the sea,
> His wings truly earned, and name—Red Devil.

Chapter Eight
Arnhem

On returning to England, my 1st Battalion was stationed at Grimsthorpe Castle, Bulby Hall and Bourne in Lincolnshire. The 2nd Battalion was at Stoke Rochford Hall, near Grantham, and the 3rd at Spalding. Initially, 1st Battalion C.O. was Lieutenant-Colonel Cleasby-Thompson, who had succeeded Jock Pearson after the Sicily Landings. We would miss Jock Pearson. But then we had another change in command when Cleasby-Thompson was succeeded by Lieutenant-Colonel K.T. Darling, and then another only a month later when Darling was relieved by Lieutenant-Colonel David Dobie from the 3rd Parachute Battalion. Colonel Dobie was an experienced Para and a likeable man who informed us that he would train us from 'A' to 'Z', and he did just that.

All over the country things were working up to a terrific pitch in preparation for the Second Front and for several months we carried out exercises in near combat conditions. We were briefed for numerous operations that somehow didn't get off the ground—one near Paris codenamed 'Transfiguration', another near Caen codenamed 'Wild Oats', and yet another codenamed 'Comet', involving the Albert Canal in Belgium. Something really big was in the air and in August men coming from our old training area of Tatton Park reported seeing thousands of tanks there, 'like a giant tank park'.

Sure enough, in mid-September we were finally setting off somewhere. I checked over my gear: one Gammon bomb, two .36 hand grenades, combined pick and shovel, webbing equipment with small pack, two ammunition pouches and bandolier with .303 ammunition, water bottle, mess tin, iron ration, field dressing, camouflage net scarf, triangle-shape air recognition bright yellow silk scarf—tied around the neck ready for instant use—rifle, and an escape kit comprising of a silk map of Europe, a small button compass and a strong file the size of a nail file. That was about it, except for a kit bag strapped to the leg and a parachute, plus Mae West life jacket in case we finished up in the drink. I felt like an overdue pregnant hippo and didn't know where to put anything else, though still added two hundred cigarettes, two bars of chocolate and some boiled sweets.

I wondered how the rest of the men were going to fare on this hop. I was just getting used to the new faces, like Frankie (Panzer) Manser, Bill Silbery, Terry Brace, Dick Bingley, Dolly Gray, Major Perrin-Brown, Sid Oxley, Guv Beech (with his top hat—the Germans will surrender in surprise if he takes that with him, I thought), Joe McCready, Paddy McCormack, and Captain Joe Gardiner. Unfortunately, Sergeant Busty Everett had fallen ill and died at Bourne. We were from all over the country and beyond, and on the whole one big happy family.

It was daylight when we clambered into trucks and headed to the Aerodrome at Barkston Heath. Everyone was tense but ready to go, come what may. Huddled in the curtained trucks, covered from view for security reasons, men chatted and smoked, and minds wandered. Then someone started humming, more joined in, and some raunchy alternative words to the tune of the old Irish folk ditty 'My Brother Sylvest' filled the air:

My brother Sylvest
Can do any turn like the rest.
'E can run, jump, fight, f**k,
Wheel a barrer, push a truck,
Turn a double somersault
An' whistle with 'is arse-ole.
That's my brother Sylvest!

At the aerodrome everyone was waiting calmly but with an eagerness to get going. On airfields all over the south and east of England men were assembling to be taken by glider or plane and, as we were shortly to learn, set down or dropped in enemy-occupied Holland. Our objective was to capture and hold the bridge straddling the Rhine at Arnhem. My 1st Parachute Battalion was to seize the high ground to the north.

At last, amid the roar of engines warming up, I heard the order to prepare to emplane. I was number 13 in the 93rd aircraft in the third wave to take off, and scheduled to drop in enemy territory at 15.00. I was not superstitious but having the number 13 did make me think! The C47 Dakota was now roaring down the runway. I thought that it would not make it, but somehow, after the point of no return, it lifted in time. We circled around for an hour, manoeuvring into a mass formation before setting course for Holland. It was a great sight seeing all those planes, and gave a sense of security that one was not alone on this mission. Being a few thousand feet up, it was hard to recognize the scenery below, but as we approached the south coast I saw the familiar Thames Estuary as we flew over my home county of Kent. Then we were past Dover and heading for the Dutch coast.

Our escorting Typhoon, Spitfire and Mustang fighters were weaving between the Dakotas and gliders, and as we crossed the English Channel tension began to mount in my plane. We approached land on the other side and could see that the area had been flooded to try and stop or impede the advance of our land forces. I was admiring the landscape when the order rang out: 'Action stations! Hook Up! Green light on! Go!' Being number 13, I had a few long seconds to wait as I shuffled forward. Then I felt a slight pat on my parachute pack and again found myself tumbling out of the doorway into that familiar open void.

My parachute once more obediently opened and I drifted down to earth without difficulty. After a good three-point landing I was now in enemy-occupied territory. Except for occasional machine gun fire and some blasting from enemy gun emplacements, the landing had been unopposed and the whole dropping zone north of Heelsum was packed with gliders and discarded parachutes. Everyone soon collected themselves and rendezvoused at their respective points. The time was just after 15.00 on Sunday the 17th of September 1944.

The 1st Airborne Landings continued to go reasonably well, with progress gathering momentum towards the intended goal: the bridge at Arnhem. The drop zone was like a giant intersection, Jeeps calmly bouncing over the plough. Gliders were coming in to land like an inter-city air service. Soldiers were collecting equipment from containers and then sprinting off to join up with their respective units, earmarked by various coloured smoke canisters.

My 1st Para Battalion, codenamed 'Leopard', made for the northerly route above Wolfheze. Meanwhile, the 2nd Para Battalion, codenamed 'Lion', under Colonel Frost, set off along the lower and southerly route, below Oosterbeek, to push on as fast as possible to the bridge. The 3rd Para Battalion, codenamed 'Tiger', under Colonel Finch, was to take the route directly through Oosterbeek. We had been told to expect limited enemy resistance and did not know at the time there was a formidable formation of German SS troops just north of the Utrecht-Arnhem road.

Leaving the drop zone, we made our way along a track running alongside the woods west of Wolfheze and south of the railway. The end of the track linked up with a road running parallel to the railway. Turning right here, and then over the road on to the railway sidewalk, we nosed our way towards Wolfheze Station. Suddenly, there was a loud explosion up ahead and some machine gun fire. Stopping awhile, I kept my eyes on the woods to our right and the railway track running from east to west. We moved on, the leading Company—'R' Company, under Major John Timothy—meeting with hit and run jabs from the enemy. Mortar bombs were whining and bullets slashed the undergrowth as we pushed on hard. Nearing the station, by a rail crossing over the road, we came upon a knocked-out flak gun, the crew sprawled grotesquely around its perimeter. There were a number of bomb craters and smashed buildings, including an asylum in ruins, some of whose occupants were roaming about in a daze. This was the aftermath of the Allied bombing. The smell of war was really beginning to circulate in my nostrils now.

Turning left at the rail crossing, we headed towards the Ede-Arnhem road. 'R' Company, still up front, became engaged in a fierce battle, facing armoured cars, mortars and machine guns. It was getting dark now. The whole Battalion lay doggo for a while to try to avoid further detection. We lay up in the woods for some hours, pushing on occasionally but cautiously. At one time, unbeknown to the enemy, they completely surrounded us. I could see the silhouettes of German infantry ambling around their half-track vehicles, but after a while they left the area and we pressed on again.

Occasional enemy small arms fire helped to smother any noise we may have been making, but we came to another sudden halt in response to more small arms and mortar fire at close range, soon quelled by the quick action of our forward companies. We hadn't gone all that far but it was rough and tedious going. In the semi-dark we passed down winding lanes, through woods, and then along the south side of the Ede-Arnhem road. We were now about five miles from the Arnhem Bridge and so far luck had been with us.

Keeping cover along avenues of trees off the road, we were halted again by the leading scout just short of the main road. Just as well too, because up and down the road, cruising undecidedly, was a large number of German SP (self-propelled) guns, not more than 80 feet away from us. The Battalion lay doggo again and watched this display of German armour. We had no choice but to pause, as to take on this little lot would have meant slaughter for us. After an uneasy hour, lying up quietly but ready for anything, we moved off again, groping our way through the thick wooded country in the dark. It was most disconcerting and everything seemed too calm.

At about 02.00 there were sounds of battle ahead, apparently coming from the area north-northeast of Lichtenbeek. On arriving there at about 05.00 we found that the leading companies had met fierce opposition and had suffered heavily. Then, with no reason given at the time, the original plan to go for the high ground north of Arnhem was changed and we instead turned south towards Mariendaal and Oosterbeek, some two miles from the bridge.

At 06.00 we entered Oosterbeek, where we met members of the Dutch Underground Movement who showed us the easiest route to the bridge. We were moving cautiously in file ready for action and everything still seemed a bit too quiet. At 06.30, as dawn was breaking, we moved into a built-up area and then it started. The enemy had been busy overnight, preparing gun emplacements, taking up positions at vantage points, posting snipers, and concealing tanks and SP Guns. German gunfire shattered the peace and I darted for cover and took up position in the neatly laid out garden of a nearby house. More firing came from the house direction. With two other men I ran round the back of the house and fired at two Germans in the shrubbery. They must have had their chips. Amid the smoke and fire of machine guns, SP guns and six-barrelled mortars, the battle raged and built to such a pitch that I became quite accustomed to it and went about the task as if on street-fighting training back home.

We hadn't eaten since leaving England but I was too busy to be hungry. Casualties were mounting incredibly fast and in every direction I could see the motionless forms of our men cut down in their tracks. Progress was slow and the battle became more intense as the bridge loomed gradually nearer. At a point south between Den Brink and St. Elisabeth's Hospital, at a factory area near the river, we came under heavy machine gun fire and mortaring.

With two other chaps I did not know, I chased after some Germans in a house. We threw in a grenade and dashed through the door to finish them off with Sten and rifle. Looking around for any more of the enemy, we belted to the rear of the house. I tripped over a broken fence and went sprawling. As I scrambled up I heard a close whine, which I recognized as a mortar. I dived for cover by a low wall and the bomb landed very near, near enough to feel the draught. Snipers were taking pot shots at us. Dodging and weaving through gardens and back yards, I came to a stop opposite a factory, held up by heavy mortar and machine gun fire yet again. I threw myself to the ground. It was absolute bedlam, with the slicing sound of German Solothurn guns, their bullets cutting the air in every direction, and the repeated *stonk* of mortars, followed by the whine and sound of hot shrapnel hitting rooftops. A small lump of shrapnel hit my helmet, sounding like a pea on a drum.

In the heat of the battle men were shouting curses, lobbing grenades through open doors and windows, and following up with shrieks of contempt for the enemy and the cry of 'Who-oooh-Mohamed'. Casualties were really mounting. There were groans from men who had been hit. Motionless Paras lay in the road and slumped over walls. I saw a pair of feet protruding from a garden gateway, one boot blown off but leaving the foot complete, such was the magical phenomenon of war.

The German firepower was murderous and all I could do was keep alert for the sound of English. I had a horrible feeling that my Battalion was being cut to ribbons. Fire was coming from my left from behind a row of houses and from the rooftops and windows. At the same time, SP gun, mortar and machine gun fire was coming from my front, from the direction of the hospital. To my right was a wool factory, with the river and a brick works beyond. A couple of shots came my way, very close. Someone was trying to single me out and I thought I'd make for the factory. I heaved into a crouching position and catapulted forward like an Olympic runner, zigzagging for twenty paces before hitting the ground and rolling sideways, coming to a stop with a bump at the corner of the factory. Peering cautiously around it in the direction of the river, I noticed our men charging on and quickly slipped around and out of the line of fire of the bastard to my left who was trying to get me.

It crossed my mind that maybe fifth columnists were busy. We knew that quite a few members of the Dutch National Socialist Party were in the area, working in cooperation and collaborating with the Germans. None had been caught red-handed, but on entering the outskirts of Arnhem early that morning we had been warned by the Dutch Resistance to be wary of them. Taking up a position by the factory with my back to the river, I was now firing at Germans who appeared at windows, from behind chimney pots, and even in trees. They were cunning, strapping themselves to the trees so that when hit they would not fall to the ground and give their positions away.

There was a heck of a battle going on inside the factory and men were scrapping furiously with grenades, Stens, Colt handguns and fighting knives. The wall of the house opposite received a blast of machine gun fire coming from behind me. I was about to move off in pursuit of a German in the garden of a terraced house on my right when I felt an explosion just beneath me, and a sharp pain. Reeling over and looking down, I saw that the lower part of my right leg was in a most unusual position and blood was oozing out steady and fast. I shouted for help and two Paras dashed up and quickly rendered first aid. One of them, Sergeant Nobby Hall, called for a medical orderly. I was worried, but felt a nuisance too as everyone was busy enough already without being lumbered with me. I was placed on a stretcher and carried to a wooden shed a few yards away, where medics cut the boot from the foot of my shattered leg, smashed by an explosive bullet. It looked awful but, strangely, I didn't feel much pain. They tore open the field dressing I had carried for so long in different parts of the world but never previously needed, and carried out a quick but thorough job.

Pandemonium was reigning outside as machine gun fire echoed around the built up area. A mortar bomb landed quite near, but the medic administering a morphine injection kept as steady a hand as if in the safety of a hospital back in England. While the other medic hunted around for a suitable makeshift splint, a young Dutch girl appeared from nowhere and offered me a welcome cup of water. I was feeling cold and clammy and her help was a great comfort, as was the morphine, which soon began to take effect.

There was another series of explosions just ahead, a clear signal to get moving, and I was carried cautiously to the corner of a house next to the road I had come down only a short while ago. Everyone was scattered and there were dead Paras in the road, on the sidewalk and in gardens. Snipers were busy and our men were bent on winkling them out. There was a thud, a whiz, and the bark of an exploding shell, followed by another, and another, all bursting on the rooftops of houses thirty yards back. Then something flashed from an upper window only twenty yards ahead and bullets splattered the wall above us. The medics set me down to wait for an opportune moment to get across the road and I saw four Paras press themselves into the wall of the building opposite as they worked their way towards that flash. When under the window, the leading Para kicked the door and out of the window came a 'potato masher', which he immediately picked up and threw back in, accompanied by a Mills bomb thrown by another man. There was quite some explosion, following which the four Paras entered the building, spraying Sten gun fire in the room and up through the floorboards, a trick we had learned in training. A Schmeisser automatic fell from the top window, closely followed by an SS man. The medics grabbed my stretcher and crossed the road.

I was more than relieved to get out of the line of fire and was carried to the relative safety of a garden wall. As I lay helpless behind the wall I had a clear view of the clatter and confusion of battle through the demolished gateway. I saw four of our men in a Jeep, who thought they would run the gauntlet and belted by, accelerating and swerving wildly, guns blazing. They must have been doing 40 miles per hour and the driver was fighting with the wheel as he dodged shell bursts and potholes in the road, veering from one side to the other and bouncing over obstacles. Hurtling around a dead Para spread-eagled in the road, the Jeep came to a halt so vigorously that the four occupants literally flew out. Unscathed, they picked themselves up and disappeared into the brick and concrete jungle, leaving a now hissing Jeep with a broken front wheel pinion. A few moments later a mortar volley descended around the vehicle, instantaneously enveloping it in flames.

I was moved with a number of other wounded men to a nearby barn, where I spent a fairly easy night thanks to the powerful effects of the morphine injection I had been given. Early the following morning all was reasonably quiet in the immediate vicinity, although I could hear the sound of battle not far off. Looking around the barn, I didn't recognise anyone from my 1st Battalion and those men I spoke to did not want to know—they were either too preoccupied with their wounds or unable to talk at all. Some of them looked as though they had just had a nightmare.

Medical orderlies were busy with Jeeps, shuttling the wounded back up the road to Oosterbeek. It was impossible to get through to St. Elisabeth's Hospital as German armour was blocking all the approaches. My leg was beginning to give me a bit of hell now and movement of any sort was painful. At about 07.00 two medics came up to me and said that it was my turn next. Lifting the stretcher, they carried me to a waiting Jeep, its engine running. There were four walking wounded in the back seats and I was strapped to the front of the bonnet alongside another chap who was already strapped on beside the windscreen. He forced a grin. 'What's yours?' I asked. 'They got me in the guts', he said bluntly. That's a nasty place to cop it, I thought, feeling sorry for him. I wondered how all my friends were getting on. Had they made it to the bridge? Were any of them wounded or killed? There was a strong possibility.

A short stocky medic jumped into the driver's seat, saying, 'hold tight in the back, and don't worry you two in front on the bonnet. We might have a rough ride and will be going a bit fast'. As we started off, I had the horrible feeling that being right at the front I would crash into whatever obstacle happened to suddenly loom up, but the lad managed to miss them all. En route, enemy machine gunners decided to open up on us, even though we were flying a Red Cross flag. I was worried in case I got hit again. The driver and sitting wounded in the back did their best to make themselves as small as possible but the two of us strapped to the bonnet had to take pot luck.

After a fast and bumpy journey, the Jeep tore through Oosterbeek, past Divisional Headquarters at the Hartenstein Hotel, and pulled up sharply in the drive of the Tafelberg Hotel a few hundred yards farther on. Airborne medics quickly unstrapped me and took me inside, setting me down on the floor opposite a window in the entrance hall. Looking around, I saw two wounded Germans among our own men and some Dutch civilians who had been caught up in the battle. One of the Germans looked at me and said something I didn't understand. An orderly told me he was enquiring after my health'. 'Tell him to get knotted', I said. 'I'm not in the mood for niceties'.

Chapter Nine
The Hotel Tafelberg

The Hotel Tafelberg had been German Field Marshall Walther Model's headquarters prior to our arrival on the previous Sunday and we were now using it as an improvised military hospital. It must have taken a few knocks, as it was now an absolute shambles. As usual, the British Tommy had managed to brew up even in such hazardous conditions and I was given a mug of tea and a bar of chocolate—my first food since leaving England two days earlier. I had still not touched my ghastly iron ration. I tried to sleep, but the interruption of shelling and mortar fire prevented that. When night fell I just longed for daylight to come again. I hated the nights. It was bad enough meeting angry Germans in battle, but it was worse to do so while I slept.

The next day, Wednesday, I was grateful to be taken to the operating room, ingeniously rigged up in the kitchen of the hotel. Work was made very difficult for the medical staff but under the guidance of Colonel Graeme Warrack, the ADMS (Assistant Director Medical Services), conditions were overcome for a while and the surgeon, Major Guy Rigby Jones, operated on my leg as well as could be expected under extreme circumstances. Captain Michael James, the other surgeon, had been badly hurt when a shell landed a few feet from the foot of the stairs just before I arrived. Wounded along with his team, he became another resident casualty, later telling me that they were in the entrance hall when the shell had burst and he was blown right through the double spring doors into the main ward—the dining room before the battle. When he got up to return to the hall he could see nothing but dust and smoke and had to get his own bleeding stopped and attend to his team members, after which he vaguely remembers trying to visit patients upstairs, but could not make it for long because of his wounds.

I was returned to the entrance hall, where the din of battle and bullets hitting the wall outside made me look out. I was surprised to see a German wandering about. He took up a stand position by the door, and then began pacing up and down. All sorts of stuff was being flung our way and the medics thought it best to move some of us up to the next floor. A chap named Bannister, together with William Roberts of the 16th Para Field Ambulance, hastily picked up my stretcher and began to haul me up the wide and littered stairway. Just then there was a loud *crump* outside and debris, plaster and glass fell all around. I looked to see where that one had landed and the German I had seen outside only a few moments ago was now sprawled out, killed I presume by one of his own mortar bombs.

I was set down at the head of the stairs. To my right lay a glider pilot who had a face and arm injury. Amid all the wounded, who covered most of the landing area, came a wounded man walking. Our eyes met. Did I know him? I hardly knew anyone. They were unrecognizable, clotted up with blood and dirt. He said he was from 1st Battalion's 'R' Company. 'I got my lot near Mariendaal', he told me. 'What about your company commander Major Timothy?' I asked. 'Dunno!' he snapped. 'They're getting bloody cheeky with their muck slinging.' Then, up the stairs belted some combat Paras and we asked them how it was going. 'Not too bad, not too bad, could be better', one said, before disappearing back down again.

Although my leg was giving me a lot of pain now, this was offset somehow by all the activity around me. One lad was calmly going around brewing tea, and the medics, as ever, were continuing to do a grand job despite the appalling conditions. Ann Pelster Caspers, one of the Dutch nurses, came by with an armful of sheets and curtain material for use as bandages, which partially hid her blood stained apron. The smell of death was all around, together with body odour caused through lack of washing. One became strangely accustomed to both.

A wounded man with his arm in a sling approached me with an enquiring look. 'What unit, chum?' he asked almost in a whisper. 'First Para', I replied, amid a shower of dust and smoke, as yet another shell exploded very near. He winced and withdrew from the direction of the shell blast, just as we felt the ominous vacuum of warm air. He was almost incoherent as he glanced around the terrible scene of man-made destruction. 'I just left the bridge', he said. There was quite a pause. 'What's it like there?' I asked. He swung around glaring at me as if the whole war was my fault, his eyes hard, staring and red with fatigue. The poor fellow had been through something bad. I offered him a cigarette, and with a trembling hand he took one. It hung limp in his grasp. 'Thanks. I don't really smoke, but I'll have one', he said. Then he answered: 'It was bloody hell there. Tanks belching fire, blokes getting killed right and left. The carnage was terrible.' He paused as a medic passed by with a man clutching his side and hobbling on one leg, a bloody congealed bandage wrapped around the stump where once had been a foot. My lad drew hard on his cigarette and, coughing, continued: 'There were hordes of them; it went on for hours—attacking, shelling; then the bastards started burning us out. My two mates got killed. The twisted and broken bodies of our men were strewn everywhere.' He leaned back against the wall looking a little more at ease. I don't know, but I think I may have been the first person he had spelt out his experiences to. Later he told me that it was his first time in action. I thought he had ridden it bloody well.

The next few days seemed to drag on forever, with my leg giving me much more pain now than it had during the first 24 hours after I was hit. The morphine injection must have worn off and the pain was excruciating—like someone making a short sharp jab with a knife with a blunt serrated edge. Momentarily, the agony was dispersed with the thundering crash of a shell landing downstairs. It sounded much too near for the comfort of the wounded down there. For all the humding that was going on inside we might just as well have been outside. There were so many shells landing in, on, and around the building, plus the occasional burst of machine gun fire spattering the inner walls, that I imagined we must be slap bang in the front line or somewhere in no-man's land.

The Dutch doctor Gerrit van Maanen and his 17-year-old daughter Anje and son Paul were doing an extraordinary job in what were now the ruins of this once-quiet hotel. There was a sudden flurry of activity as Anje and Paul, together with Ann Pelster Caspers and two medics, made a dash down the stairs to receive two Jeeps packed with walking wounded from the perimeter area. There were hundreds of wounded, enemy included, as well as Dutch people caught up in the fight—so many that some got moved to the hotel's annexe across the driveway—and any man with flesh wounds or injuries that did not hinder the use of a firearm was ordered outside to fight.

It was now Saturday the 23rd of September and I was still lying at the head of the broad stairway when there was a commotion down below. 'Those ruddy Huns again!' said the glider pilot. There was a shuffling and German orders were being rapped out, then some SS troops dashed up the stairs. A sinister-looking type, about twenty years old, led the way and was coming right at me. I found myself looking straight down the barrel of his Schmeisser, his trigger finger shaking. I didn't bat an eyelid—I just did not want to upset him and give him cause to let rip. He was glaring at me with red beady eyes. Christ, this is it, I thought. I had heard of other wounded being shot up. But my luck was in, and he passed me by. He and two other SS men had a good look around and then took up firing positions at windows in rooms leading off the landing. As they started to fire out, Colonel Warrack dashed up the stairs, swearing and rebuking them for firing from a clearly marked Red Cross building. Discipline took over: they looked defiant and sullen, but with fingers handling their automatics hesitantly, they reluctantly obeyed the officer's command and stopped firing. They paced up and down, glaring at everyone, then started scrounging for cigarettes, trying each man in turn. One came up to me and interrupted my unpleasant thoughts of him: 'Zigaretten?' I had 200 tucked under the blanket and bandage to my leg. 'No, mate' was my innocent reply, or was I trying to needle him? His piercing pale blue eyes were studying the half-smoked cigarette in my hand. 'Vot is dat?' 'Oh, that's a dog-end'. He was getting a bit edgy. 'Vot is dock ent?' 'It's a doofer, mate—doofer-nother-day'. He shrugged his shoulders and sloped off. After a very short while he and his friends were all gone and our own men were back in charge. It was most strange to have the enemy in the building one minute, only to be replaced by our own combat men the next.

I wondered how the rest of my 1st Para Battalion were doing. Right from the Sunday night our 'R' Company had had a tough time, losing half its men in the 'De Leeren Doedle' area. Then, forty men of 6 Platoon, 'S' Company were killed in two minutes in the Mariendaal district on the approach to Arnhem, and in the Den Brink, St. Elisabeth's Hospital and factory area of Klingelbeekseweg (where I was hit) the rest of the Battalion was badly mauled. Here in the Tafelberg the conditions for the medical people must have been exasperating, as water and lighting were almost non-existent, although an electrician from Oosterbeek did manage to keep the electric and water supply going for a while. Our medics had been unable to carry out any operations since Wednesday because of the pounding the building was taking from shellfire and medical instruments were buried in deep debris.

Now, the medics were tending to men who had been wounded for a second time whilst inside the hotel. Across the landing I noticed a Dutch girl, Atie Schultz, doing her best to comfort a young Para who had been hit in the guts. In the midst of it all, Father Benson, a Roman Catholic priest, was busy making his rounds and answering urgent calls—one man so constantly needed. Things began to get on my nerves that morning, what with the continuous din of battle outside and my leg getting more painful through lack of proper medical attention. I called for Father Benson to offer a few words of comfort, so he came and put me at my ease. Later, he too was wounded by tank fire into the building. I am sorry to say that he died from those wounds and was buried in the grounds of St Elisabeth's Hospital.

On the following day the disposition was frightening. Our men were still doing their damnedest but the Germans were slowly closing in—very slowly, mark you, for they lost heavily and had to fight hard for every inch of that bloody ground out there. With things getting hotter still, I was moved again to what was thought to be a safer spot—just to the other side and along the landing area. It felt great to be moved, if only a few yards, and it gave me a new lease of life. I took in the scenery about me. Every bit of floor space was packed with wounded, with just enough room for the medical people to pick a way through.

Suddenly, there was an almighty explosion in a room on my right. Men already wounded, once, twice, were hit again and some were killed. There were piteous cries coming from that room. It was at this time that Major John Waddy of the 156th Parachute Battalion, who had started his parachuting days in India when the battalion was first formed, was wounded again and two English medics and a Dutch nurse were killed. A medic now came out cradling a form in his arms. The chap he carried could have been dead or unconscious—he was covered in blood and his arm was shattered and hung pathetically by his side, his left leg bandaged from his first wounding. The medic faltered, eyes red, face drawn and dust-covered, his whole frame crying out with gross fatigue. Bracing himself, he picked his way through the men on the floor. Unwittingly his foot came into contact with a man's hand. 'Sorry lad', he said. 'S'all right', was the reply, and then the man slid off in a coma.

Christ, I wished I were outside. There was another resounding crash of bombs, followed by curses. Perhaps I was better off in here. It was bloody awful for everyone everywhere. A medic picked his way past me, a lonely man among hundreds of wounded. I tugged at his trousers and he stopped immediately. 'What's up, lad?' I was shaking and felt a coward bothering him. Almost pleading, I asked, 'What's going on out there?' He put a hand on my shoulder: 'Those shells are ours', he said. 'That's 30 Corps medium artillery at Nijmegen.' I breathed a sigh of relief—I had thought they were enemy shells.

Outside, the situation was getting completely out of hand. Further enemy reinforcements were mustering around the perimeter in the form of powerfully armed tanks from the SS Panzer divisions with long-barrelled high explosive and armour-piercing shells. The passage where I lay ran from front to rear of the hotel, and I was facing the rear, with a grandstand view of the battle through a gaping hole in the wall where once had been a window. Now and again one of our men would break cover to stalk the enemy, and then the enemy would repeat the process, with the multiple accompaniment of shell burst, tank fire, machine gun fire, curses and yelps of pain.

I heard the ominous sound of an approaching tank. I couldn't see it, but the squeaking of its caterpillar wheels grew ever louder. Then it came into view, its great gun traversing from right to left. Picking its way through the trees, it stopped for a few minutes to feel its way, and then the gun barked out, sending a shell across my front to an unseen target. There were some of our anti-tank guns in the vicinity and maybe it was after them. The tank was approximately 150 yards away and heading in my direction, stopping periodically and rotating its gun turret. It crept forward to about 100 yards, then—I went quite cold—its gargantuan barrel slewed round and came to rest pointing right at me. The gun bellowed out. I froze and shut my eyes. I don't know whether the shell passed through the building via the gaping holes already made by shellfire or passed very close outside, but I felt the draught as it sailed by. Sod that, I thought, and looked around for someone to move me to a safer place.

The other wounded were lying huddled together trying to afford each other protection. The floor was littered with debris, blood and glass, and there was an incessant whine and explosion of mortar bombs, together with the shriek and crash of artillery vibrating the very foundations of the building, which I thought would at some point tumble down. The place was now barely recognisable as a hotel. A Dutch civilian sidled by, gingerly picking his way through the wounded, giving apologetic gestures. 'Who's he?' I asked a medic. 'That's Mr. Bouwman', he said. 'He and his family, with a ten-year-old son, have been in the cellar ever since we arrived'.

I don't know what time it was when the shelling and gunfire stopped, but after the din of the last six days it felt very strange to suddenly be so much quieter. There was still spasmodic firing in the distance and a little shelling, but nothing to worry about. We began to converse more freely. 'Gone on strike, Jerry?' one man almost shouted, except that he had half his mouth bandaged from a shell splinter wound. 'Nah, 'ees packed up, 'as Jerry, an' buggered orf!' a cockney put in. The glider pilot was more cautious: 'Crafty sod is the Hun. He's got something up his sleeve!' Then I saw men being carried downstairs, with great activity going on outside, but not of battle. Two medics picked me up, both of them silent and not looking too pleased. 'Where to now?' I asked. 'The Elisabeth Hospital', one told me. The enemy had overrun us and was calling the shots.

Chapter Ten
One Hospital to Another

Outside was a ghastly sight, with the dead of both sides still lying where they had fallen. British and German medical orderlies were putting the wounded into Jeeps and various other vehicles, including two small vans improvised as makeshift ambulances. Three of us stretcher cases were loaded on to a small open German lorry with shallow sides, which would prevent us bouncing off in transit. There was just enough room also for five walking wounded. Anje Maanen, Ann Pelster Caspers and Atie Schultz were still there, working to the end and trying their best to make things more bearable for everyone.

We set off, the journey made more difficult because of the shell-holed and litter-strewn road. Fortunately, the German driver couldn't go too fast but he was still rather erratic in negotiating heaps of debris from gutted buildings, partially destroyed by shellfire. The dead littered the road and sidewalk all the way to St. Elisabeth's Hospital and knocked-out equipment was heaped everywhere. We all had shattered bones of some sort, which made us cry out in pain during the rough ride in this antiquated lorry and I was more than pleased when it finally came to a standstill at journey's end.

At the hospital there had clearly been heavy fighting as spent cartridge cases could be seen littering the floor and entranceway. I heard the familiar voice of a friend: 'What the hell are you doing on that stretcher— scrounging a lift?' I went to answer but nothing came out. It was not the remark; I couldn't care less; it was that ride from the Tafelberg. Sam Coster was discussing the battle with someone, a medic, I think: 'The Poles had a rough passage—only 200 got over to us', he said, 'and the Lonsdale Force had their hands full too'. That was the force formed by Major Dickie Lonsdale of the 11th Para Battalion when things went drastically wrong in the early stages. Made up of units left from the 1st and 4th Para Brigades, Sam and a few others from my 1st Battalion had numbered in it.

Word got around that the whole show was over and I began to wonder what had really gone wrong. I learnt that on the day of our arrival a nationwide railway strike had started in Holland, and also that the Germans had re-flooded the area south of the Arnhem Bridge during the battle to try to prevent a link-up with us from Nijmegen. I hoped that Alan Wood, the Daily Express reporter, and Stanley Maxted from the BBC, who had both been in the Oosterbeek perimeter area, had made it out to tell the tale. The battle had been lost but it had been some fight. As mortar sergeant Dick Whittingham later wryly remarked, 'We may have lost the battle at Arnhem, but we did come in second!' It should be noted that there had been not only great loss of life in this battle but also massive local destruction, with one in four houses in Wolfhezen, Oosterbeek and Arnhem totally destroyed and most of the remainder badly damaged.

I had been lying on the same stretcher since the previous Monday week but now found myself in a bed with white sheets and was given a good bed bath. I was put on some sort of diet, consisting of pease pudding, milk pudding, soup and dark brown bread, with butter made from coal. It was tasteless but edible. There was a German nun with an infernal blank expression gliding from bed to bed with a basket of bread, droning, 'brude,

brude'. I wondered if living under the religious vows of her convent and being German had any bearing on her feelings towards the devastations of war. It did not seem to show. If only she could just grimace or partially smile.

The hospital was now choc-a-bloc with wounded. When the Germans were preoccupied, many of the fit, or fitter, men among us were nipping over the wall, assisted by members of the Dutch Underground Movement, who at great risk to themselves did much to help. I spoke to the man next to me but he didn't answer. He was miles away or did not want to know. He had one leg off and one in plaster. On my other side, a chap had a leg amputation and flesh wounds to his left arm. 'If it's not a stupid question', I said, 'how are you?' He turned slowly, and with a hoarse voice answered: 'Except for shrapnel in my arm, a leg missing and a splitting headache, I'm OK. I suppose I'm lucky to be alive.' Then a British Tommy with no Para gear hobbled by, a bloody bandage wrapped around his head. 'What mob are you?' I asked (my first thought was of spies in our midst). 'The Dorsets!' he almost cried. 'My lot were wiped out.' I later heard that two companies of the Dorsets from the 43rd Division had crossed the Rhine and made it to the 1st Airborne Division perimeter in Oosterbeek—most likely the only outside force that managed to get to us.

My leg was giving me hell now, and was getting worse every hour, but I had to wait until the most serious cases had been seen to. Medical orderlies were constantly up and down the ward tending the wounded, and you could hear whispered calls of 'medic, help me'. A passing medic would console or administer any medical treatment within his power or learning, and be called again and again before disappearing through the door, only to reappear as a stretcher-bearer with yet another battered body. Along with the civilian nurses, these wonderful people were everyone's absolute comforters. Some of the nurses were quite good looking and made men ogle, but any other feelings I might have had were kept in check by the thought that they could be planted Gestapo agents exercising all their charms, including showing a little extra cleavage, in an attempt to extract information.

To my right rear was a door leading off the main ward to a small corridor where various stores and private rooms were situated. In one of these, away from German scrutiny, was Brigadier John Hackett, the 4th Para Brigade Commander, who had been badly wounded in Oosterbeek. To mislead the Germans as to his true rank he was posing as a lance corporal, which just goes to show that lance corporals have other uses!

I was brought back to my own discomfort by a sharp pang of a thousand knives, caused by the throbbing puss-filled wound of my leg. I was now getting most concerned. Since being hit I'd had nothing apart from morphine jabs and reassuring words. At last the medics came for me—I don't know when exactly, as day and night had become one big nightmare in my private agony. 'OK, feller, we're going to make you comfortable now', I heard. 'You'll be fine in no time, you'll see.' Oh sweet bloody words. Let's get cracking then. I don't know where they took me. Things were happening fast. It was a haze of walls and doors swinging open, the soft sound of nurses and nuns as they whisked by on their next mission of mercy, the unnecessary clatter of boots as the SS guards gloated over the suffering of the wounded, plus the screech of our artillery shells, with their subsequent *crump* as they landed nearby.

A South African orthopaedic surgeon, Captain Alexander Lipmann-Kessel, was going to see me. He commanded one of the surgical teams of 16 Para Field Ambulance. I was thankful that I was not going to have a German butcher. I had seen the end result of a German doctor's amputation of a man's foot, crudely almost guillotined, and without anaesthetic. I was carried into a large room with medical apparatus everywhere—trolleys and tables laden with all sorts of instruments, bandages, field dressings and splints. I was placed on a hard, narrow table about four feet from the ground. In the distance I could hear the sound of gunfire and German flak, which meant that our aircraft were in the vicinity. The anaesthetist had his needle at the ready and medics were preparing for the operation when there was a noise rather like a giant balloon having air released, and then a terrific explosion. With very quick presence of mind one medic threw a blanket over me and shielded me from the blast with his own body as shattered glass fell in small pieces and slivers all over the operating theatre. Then all went quiet again and the blanket was pulled carefully off to reveal yours truly with popping eyes. A quick inspection soon assured the medics I was OK. Apparently, an RAF Typhoon had come down low to blaze his rockets at some German armour on the move in Arnhem. I can only hope that his effort was on target because my treatment had to wait another day while the place was cleaned up.

Fortunately for me, my next visit was uninterrupted. The wound was cleaned and redressed and I had my first plaster cast put on, the prelude to two weeks of itching and agony. Many of the men could get over this by ingeniously using knife, fork, spoon, pencil, or anything else at hand, to push down the side of a cast, but my luck was right out because my cast encased the whole leg, except for just the toes peeping through.

I learnt that we were all going to be moved to a place north of Arnhem called Apeldoorn, where an 'Airborne Hospital' had just been set up at a pre-war Dutch Army base, the Willem III Kaserne Barracks. Any further medical care for me would now have to wait. There was a lot of coming and going with people collecting their personal belongings in readiness for the off when I heard a commotion at the ward entrance. Looking up, I saw the effeminate SS doctor, Captain Egon Skalka, waving his gloved hand at our medics. It seemed a German general was coming from Berlin to pay us a visit. How nice. Everyone was hastily tidied up and our bedding arranged ready for inspection.

Through the doors at the end of the ward they appeared: half a dozen SS officers—uniforms a selection of blue, blue-grey, field grey, brown and black. Their accoutrements and many insignia were immaculate and their brightly polished boots more in keeping with a passing out parade than the middle of a war for their survival. As well as succeeding in looking stupid it was an unnecessary waste of time and energy. But it was their time and energy, so who cared? Heading up this amusing entourage was the visiting general himself in a very pale blue uniform with loads of silver braid and complete with a monocle. This was Obersturmbannführer Walther Harzer of the 9th SS Division, as big a square-headed German as you could ever wish to meet. Accompanying him was Captain Skalka, looking just like the sort of SS officer subsequently seen in films back home. Following up the rear, a few paces from the main party, were the accompanying sallow-faced Gestapo. One was a colour sergeant, identifiable by two pips on his left lapel, with an eagle spread and a swastika on the left arm; the other was a lance corporal, with a stripe as in the British Army, but with two short parallel stripes on the left lapel and the usual SS flash on the right. Both wore that forbidding symbol of hate in the form of an armband above the left elbow—a red background with narrow black band top and bottom, completed by a black swastika on a white circle. Together these black jack-booted individuals swaggered with a squeakiness abounding in every tread. Their belted gun-holsters, shoulder straps, black ties and peaked caps completed the all-black uniform, and with gloved hands resting on waists and thumbs hooked into belts they presented a sinister sight. There was absolute silence at the sudden entrance.

The Gestapo men had just drawn level with my bed when one of the most beautiful 'Bronx Cheers' I have ever heard vibrated from the far end of the ward whence they had come! The entourage froze momentarily, the General's left eyebrow twitching. Skalka went paler than usual and looked worried, whilst fiddling with his cuff. The other SS officers, caught completely unaware, looked slightly sheepish, not knowing how to take evasive action from the sound of a raspberry being blown in the presence of their general. The two Gestapo instinctively put their hands on their gun-holsters and were the only ones to turn in the direction of the long, loud offending sound. I watched an index finger undo a holster, making bare the brown plastic-covered plate to the handle of a Luger pistol, but even this lout had enough discipline to not be fooled by a raspberry from a British Tommy.

At the end of the ward they wheeled for the General to carry on his inspection down my side. I fixed my gaze on him until he drew level. He glanced at my cap badge and then at me, expressionless. The whole entourage stopped at the foot of my bed. I had an audience, and for the very first time a close-up of a heel-clicking German general. I was wearing my first issue red beret. It had been to Africa and Sicily with me, badge too. 'What branch of service were you?' he asked in German'. Looking him squarely in the eyes I proudly announced that I was a parachutist. 'You are going to a prisoner-of-war camp', he said, the translation provided by Captain Derek Ridler, the British Army dental officer-cum-anaesthetist, who stepped forward when he noticed that I did not fully understand the German. The General turned abruptly and carried on his way, the remainder following with an air of aloofness, while the two Gestapo men gave arrogant icy stares before departing through the doors. Outside, they all stood chatting, and then with a lot of heel clicking and Heil Hitlering, dispersed. This was the cue for various discourteous remarks and hilarious laughter among the wounded. We had had our entertainment and it was great to exercise the lungs after so much tension. I think it was the first time that a lot of us had laughed since leaving England on the 17th of September.

It was the 28th of September when German orderlies carried me out of the hospital, not so carefully as our own medics, and I had to hang on to the sides of the stretcher as we descended the stone steps at the entrance to avoid sliding off. We were put into a collection of dilapidated small grimy ambulances, or rather stacked, four to a vehicle. I was bunged down below. I don't know which was the rougher ride: from the Tafelberg to Arnhem or from Arnhem to Apeldoorn. There was endless pitching and tossing, and we had to stop for a while due to the attention of a not-so-welcome RAF Spitfire. The German orderlies buggered off until it was all over and I was glad to be in a vehicle with a red cross, although judging by the noise out there the RAF didn't completely trust the good intentions of the particular Germans transporting us.

Unscathed, we arrived at the Willem III Kaserne Barracks, which now housed the Airborne Hospital, and where we were to be guarded by SS troops. Presumably the Germans thought highly of their prisoners to continue to engage the SS as our guards. It was not exactly a four star hotel. We were given iron beds with straw-filled palliasses and the floors were dirty. There was no heating and only a meagre supply of medical necessities and food. But our walking wounded and medics soon got things organized after some tough parleying with the Germans.

Two of our wounded acted as orderlies and carried me to a small room, where they placed me on a table. My plaster and dressing were removed at considerable discomfort, though this was eased by a morphine jab halfway through. It was sheer delight to have air on my skin and to rub the dull flesh once again. But what I saw for the first time was a gaping, ghastly inflamed leg swollen up to the size of a football. 'Jesus! What the blazes can they do with that?' I asked of an orderly. 'It'll be as good as new when we've finished, mate', he said. At which a doctor, or I presume he was, entered the room, accompanied by a rottenführer of the SS Medical Corps. The stench from my wound caused disapproval on the face of the doctor and, grabbing my big toe with his fingers, he slowly raised the leg, which began to bend at the wound beneath the knee where both tibia and fibia were broken. Stopping, he peered at the wound inquisitively. 'Do you mind, that hurts', I told him. Whereupon, he simply released his hold on my leg and let it fall on to the hard table, instantly turning to go and looking me in the eyes with a sadistic expression as he did so. 'You bastard square-headed shite hawk', I said. I couldn't care less if he did understand the phrase. He just raised an eyebrow with an enquiring look and departed, while I returned to my private world of pain. Then the medics came back with that infernal SS guard and re-dressed and re-plastered my leg.

I was returned to a room housing about thirty severe cases, including an RAF chap who had been burnt. I could not converse with him as he was swathed from head to waist in bandages, with just three holes left for eyes and mouth. His flying boots and trousers were scorched. He may have been on fighters, or possibly on the re-supply run at Arnhem. One of those planes, a Dakota, had carried on in flames to the end, its pilot Flight Lieutenant D.S.A. Lord being posthumously awarded the Victoria Cross. The sole survivor had been Flying Officer Henry Arthur King, the navigator, who later reached the perimeter area at Oosterbeek.

I was at the barracks for little more than a week when one morning I was prepared for yet another move, this time a short journey to the Juliana Hospital in Apeldoorn. By way of a change, along with two other wounded men, I was to be transported by horse and cart and wondered what the mighty German Reich was coming to. It was a cold but sunny October morning and a few German infantry were on the move in motorised transport, while the Dutch people were going about their daily tasks looking drawn and bewildered. I had heard reports of a group of Dutch hostages being shot after failure to produce a work force for the German military in Apeldoorn. I glanced at a pair of elderly men who stopped and stared, probably wondering who or what we were. Still wearing our dirty, torn, blood-stained airborne smocks, we were lying on stretchers across the cart, which had no sides, the lower part of our legs covered with blankets of a low grade German Army issue, much worse and thinner than the lowest grade British Army issue. The cart's solid wheels gave no comfort whatsoever to our wounds as it clanked in a pothole or mounted a raised stone. The two German orderlies accompanying us appeared to be extremely bored.

My stay at the Juliana Hospital was going to be the longest and best as far as medical care goes. The hospital was staffed with Dutch doctors and nurses, helped by our own doctors and orderlies, and the Germans left us well alone to fend for our own medical requirements. Less proficient German doctors attended operations and showed interest in the British doctors' skills. We had adequate medical supplies for a while and the Dutch staff and visiting civilians managed to procure such luxuries as soap and toothpaste, and also English books, mainly fiction. I found these books most valuable, both to make me mentally tired so that I could sleep, and also to take my mind off the excruciating pain I was experiencing. It felt like I was wearing an iron boot and someone kept tightening and loosening a handle to it.

It was decided to apply a gadget called a Kirschner Wire Extension to my leg. As both bones were broken below the knee, the theory was to stretch the leg and try to marry the broken bones in the correct position. Under an injection of *Evipan*, a steel bar was shot through my anklebone to act as an anchor. A steel cable was then attached to the anchor and to a pulley apparatus below the foot of the bed. Weights were added each day to steadily stretch the leg, otherwise I was told I would be left with a two-inch shortening, necessitating the use of a 'club boot' at a later date, which I didn't much care for. But my general and local condition had regressed considerably and I was at my lowest ebb. I was now wishing that I could see the back of this confounded, useless lump of decaying flesh and bone. On the 19th of November I got my reluctant wish and my leg was amputated by Major Peter Smith of the 133rd Parachute Field Ambulance. As I later learnt, it was not a moment too soon. Prior to the operation I had been regarded as a hopeless case, one of those certain of not lasting. After surgery, however, I made such an amazingly quick recovery that I was back to life and sitting out of bed only a week later.

The medical orderlies could not do enough for us, from baths to fetching bed pans, carrying patients from bed to loo and back again, soothing the dying, or reading a book for those too weak or exhausted to do so for themselves. They were always on call, all hours of the day and night. I wondered when they managed to eat or sleep. I asked one who was passing with a bottle in his hand. He answered quite cheerfully: 'Oh, we get forty winks now and then, with a snack in-between!'

A Polish Para who dropped at Arnhem was opposite me in a corner of the ward. He had been cut up badly and was having a rough time. A German military clergyman kept calling to say prayers and came finally to administer the last rites. As he stood there in his dark olive green uniform, black jackboots and belt, peaked cap under his arm, I scrutinized his close-cropped bull neck and square jaw. I could not help but notice, and thought how strange, that he wore a gun holster. A man of the cloth with a pistol, and in a hospital too—what next?

Chapter Eleven
Almost Home

The Germans kept shipping us out as soon as they thought we were fit enough to travel and once again I found myself in a truck, this time heading to the rail station at Apeldoorn, where we pulled up alongside and boarded a Red Cross train. I saw that we were to be under the care of German doctors and medical staff—no wonder: the train was full of German wounded. It was a plush train and there happened to be room for a dozen of us amputation cases. I counted my blessings. Buxom, stern-looking nurses, German military medical staff and unarmed guards, all strutted about, efficiency displayed to the utmost, occasionally 'Heil Hitlering' to boost their lagging morale. There was a panic when the RAF decided to pay a visit and a flak gun alongside the train coughed out a dozen-or-so shells in very quick succession. I settled on a top bunk facing the engine, receiving disapproving looks and mutterings of 'Englische Fallschirmjager'. A German orderly handed some ersatz coffee around and a beaker was begrudgingly handed to me. It was unsweetened and black, but it was a drink.

We pulled out of Apeldoorn after dark. The journey was smooth and very comfortable. I got into conversation with two German parachutists—I say 'conversation', though neither party could understand the other, except the names of places. They may have been in Africa, as they mentioned Sousse, Tamera and Bizerte, and showed great enthusiasm when I spoke of Djebel Abiod and the Tamera Valley, where we had encountered Major Witzig's Parachute Pioneer Battalion. Even in enemy hands it's a small world!

Daylight came with a German doing his nut and shouting, 'Spitfire! Achtung! Achtung! Spitfire!' I watched a lone Spitfire turn and fly parallel to the train at about 100 feet and the same distance from the train. It was quite cheeky, I thought. The pilot was having a really close look to make sure it was a hospital train. I could clearly see his goggles and off-white scarf and felt like giving him a wave as he disappeared behind some pine trees. We were now in Germany, with snow-covered mountains and forests of fir, and log cabins dotted here and there, making it all so picturesque.

As nightfall came we halted at a dismal-looking place, a small town I think. Unfortunately, the luxury was now over and as we were ushered off the train a collection of crutches of varying length was produced and given to the leg amputees. Mine could have been six inches longer. We were handed over to a new guard and the train eased quietly out of the station. The guard beckoned us to follow him and we hobbled, slouched and limped along the unwelcome station platform, stopping at some large double doors. The guard flung open one door and in we went. It was a bare, empty room except for a big bucket, just big enough for six gallons of urine, which was precisely what it was for. The room was lofty, about twenty feet high and thirty feet square. It had most likely been a store or waiting room at one time. There were two elongated windows, about eight feet by four feet, at waist height but boarded up from the outside. With not so much as a 'goodnight', the guard slammed the door shut, the crash echoing around the room.

I gathered that we were to be here for a while, so made a recce for the most comfortable spot and saw what looked like an ideal place for a kip. It was a chimneybreast, not in use but you could see where at one time the heat from the fire had discoloured the wall. I bagged the corner of the breast, which afforded a little protection from the cold draught coming under those doors. Spotting some crummy old paper, I asked a man to kindly bung up the gap. We were all a bit under the weather, with the added unpleasantness of an amputation. One lad had an arm and a hand missing, another two arms off, and most, like myself, had lost a leg. One poor fellow was the worse for blisters on his one and only foot. We had a wounded medic with us who did all he could with minimal medical supplies. We had only paper bandages.

It was not the best of nights on that cold stone floor, but somehow I slept. Others were not so fortunate, and one chap did not even live to see the rest of the journey, remaining motionless early the next morning when we were roused by the guards. They were not immediately convinced when we told them he was 'kaput'. One guard nabbed a chap to give a hand with the bucket. He motioned him towards the edge of the platform, making signs that he should empty the contents on to the line. It had to go somewhere, though perhaps not there. We had had nothing nourishing to eat since leaving Holland over 30 hours before, except for ersatz coffee and sour-tasting dark brown bread with revolting black pudding or sausage meat. At least I had managed to save a few cigarettes and still had a smoke.

A train pulled in, creaking and hissing, carrying mainly civilians, though with a few military personnel, including sailors, so we must have been near a port. It was 08.00. As we clambered into a carriage to slump on its hard ply timber seats, I noticed they were perforated for ventilation, which brought a smile to my face. Germans needed perforated seats because of the way they sometimes farted. The hard seats, together with our overall medical condition, made the journey fatiguing. With the awful rocking of the carriage as it went over points, or when passing another train going in the opposite direction, it felt like being in a dodgem car at a fairground back home after downing eight pints. On and off all day we shunted in and out of sidings, until at last our carriage was left behind while the rest of the train went on its allotted route. After a time, a lorry turned up and we were beckoned to climb aboard.

The snow was quite thick when we pulled up at what looked like a school in a small town near Münster. Three of the Yanks and myself were told to get out, and then the lorry carried on its way, leaving us standing in the crisp snow. A voice called 'Welcome buddy, come in!' He was a big American from Indiana called Marvin Adams. Inside, he showed us to a room on the left. 'Grab yerself a palliasse an' bed down here. I'll do yours, bud', he said, looking me up and down. 'How'd yer manage that feller?' 'Put the best foot forward at the wrong time', I answered. 'Ah well, this ain't the Ritz but we have fun', he said. I wondered what he meant by that.

The room that was to be my home for the next two weeks was not too bad—about 30 feet by 15 feet, with a door at each end and five sash windows on one side looking out on to the main street. There was a grimy washroom and toilet, and an outer room or lobby leading to another room serving as a dining-cum-recreation room. On and around the wooden beds was a motley collection of occupants, including Greg Testa from Massachusetts, together with Mack, Eddie, Huff, Joe and Lloyd, all also from the US. There were some Italians who had been fighting on our side, and to my profound pleasure two other English Paras: Jim Crowe from my 1st Battalion and a Sergeant Tucker, who would later be sent off to an NCO's camp.

German guards were non-existent, except at night. As we were all severely wounded and there was thick snow outside, they were obviously not worried about a mass escape. Food was sparse but regular. There were no Red Cross parcels and what one had on arrival in the way of cigarettes or other luxuries, one hung on to. Aspirin was the strongest drug available, only paper bandages were in use and the place began to smell a little high through lack of proper medical attention. Our time was spent mainly watching the German population go about their daily jobs or observing the occasional dogfight between British and German fighter planes. Excitement rose one morning when two RAF Mosquito fighter-bombers tore over the rooftops, most likely on a hit and run raid.

We lacked positive knowledge of the current military situation and Sergeant Tucker, Jim Crowe and I talked about old times. Playing card games was a favoured pastime. Any currency was accepted as stake money but the banker had to be a bit of an interpreter and currency exchange expert as well as a shrewd diplomat because there were almost as many nationalities as players: Russian, Canadian, American, Italian, Australian, Jugoslav, French, a Dutchman in English uniform, and even a Chinese in the uniform of a Frenchman! One of the German guards in his fifties (a bod along the lines of our English Home Guard) gave us a tune on his banjo and offered his cigars around. They were the size of fat cigarettes, as strong as African French Army issue and tasted like camel shit.

One day I saw Eddie talking to a Jugoslav who could speak a little English and I edged over to them on my crutches. I'd heard a lot about these tough young partisan fighters. I instinctively put my hand out and he grasped it with his big strong hand in a grip of steel. He said he was from a village called Markonjic Grad, about 15 miles from Marshal Tito's HQ at Jajce. They had taken to the mountains soon after Germany invaded Jugoslavia in 1941 and had had to contend with wolves and bears as well as fighting Germans. Another of Tito's men joined us, while another busied himself making a meal of some salami wedged between thick slices of bread. What great deeds had these men performed, I wondered.

I felt a little weak and my stump was beginning to throb, so I worked my way back to my bed. As I did so, I saw an Italian empty his pockets with care. He had just returned from town, where he had apparently been on a work party and had bartered his cigarettes and chocolate for eggs, bacon and wine. I swapped cigarettes for bread a few times—it was quite common practice between POWs and the Germans. Sometimes men on cookhouse work would return with potatoes they had lifted, hidden in headgear or in the seam of their battle dress blouse. One lad fixed up a tight fitting 'jock strap' with a small bag attached that held two potatoes. On being frisked on one occasion he jokingly said to the guard, 'Mind my balls!' The guard saw the funny side of the remark and our friend got away with it. He nicked two pounds of potatoes that way.

I was just getting used to this place when word went round that Jerry was moving some of us, maybe for repatriation. Having only one pin, I thought I stood a good chance to be in on this. Then, early one morning, three Yanks, two Russians and myself were ushered into a truck and taken to a passenger train, in which we travelled a few miles, only to detrain again, perhaps to get another connection for our as yet undisclosed destination. The guards let us wander about a bit, which we took full advantage of. After being cooped up under one roof for a couple of weeks it was a wonderful feeling of freedom to be able to propel oneself along quite a number of yards unhindered.

Another train soon pulled in and we were directed to board. Our coach was just beyond the slope of the platform and with one leg, on crutches, this made for a difficult manoeuvre, though I made it under my own steam in the end. People in the coach looked at me as if I was some sort of weird apparition. After shunting around a bit and hitching up to another train, we rolled off again. It was dusk, cold, and pretty dismal all told. Then someone struck up with our version of *Bless 'Em All*:

Sod 'em all, sod 'em all,
The long and the short and the tall;
Sod all the sergeants and W.O. ones,
Sod all the corporals and their bastard sons;
For we're saying goodbye to them all,
As back to their billets they crawl;
You'll get no promotion this side of the ocean,
So, cheer up me lads, sod 'em all!

It seemed we had joined a group of British soldiers and this was by way of an introduction! I think we all felt a little better after that song. Even the guards showed some animation at our breaking away from the usual routine.

After jogging along for about two hours, the scenery of isolated buildings and the occasional log cabin suddenly gave way to a congested array of tall buildings, factories and large residential areas. Now there was quite a spider's web of rail lines, with a lot of rolling stock about and the fascinating tinkle, crash bang as wagons were shunted into various intersections to await their next journey. This was Bremen. We pulled in slowly, and as the train came to a stop there were the sounds of doors opening and the hustle and bustle of people getting off and making their way along the platform.

It was more like a cascade when our party left the train. We were quickly ushered down a long, wide underground passageway, a bit like the covered forecourt at Kings Cross Station, only not so lofty. I found myself in the midst of a strangely blunt and artificial scene. There were German soldiers, sailors and civilians—a glum-looking lot bent only on getting where they were going—while the railway officials and porters appeared curt and outwardly authoritative, more like visiting high-ranking officers than servants of the people. Nobody seemed aware of us, though we must have looked quite a sight.

And then it happened: the air raid warning whined out. Civilian and military personnel immediately began scurrying about, and the military, I noticed, did not hesitate to shove anyone else out of their way. The air was humming with aircraft—American Boeing B-17 Flying Fortresses—and our guards quickened their step way ahead of us, periodically turning to beckon us to hurry it up.

We entered a shelter, big enough for about a hundred people, and after a lot of pushing and shoving settled down amid glares and remarks thrown our way. I was happy to let it happen, but somehow I had been pushed and guided into a corner of the shelter away from the door. If a bomb lands too near, let the Germans take the blast and cushion any effect on us, I thought. There was a wooden bench fixed to the wall. I dropped on to it exhausted. Our three guards spread out between us and the other occupants and when the bombing started in earnest the shelter shook. I was sure that one landed close outside because I felt its draught, reminding me of being blown off my feet in North Africa, only that time it was just fifty feet away. Everyone fell silent as the drone of aircraft and the whine and crash of bombs went on with ever-increasing ferocity for a good hour before dying down to a steady drumming and the occasional distant explosion.

People began to chatter as inner fear dispersed and external bravado took over. I could hear the gnashing of teeth. Glances accompanied finger pointing in our direction. The crowd was getting restive, and then a man started pouring forth words of abuse, I'd say. A big frau, about forty years old, worked her way nearer to us until she was only a couple of feet away. I felt the moisture of her spittle as she argued with the guards about the privilege we had in being allowed to be in the same shelter as the German people. I gathered that was the crux of the matter. At this point, a heavy-booted foot came out and started propelling my way. I parried firmly with my right hand and the boot just brushed my balls, coming to a harmless glancing blow on my left thigh. The guards stood firm, restraining the woman and trying to calm everyone down. It was only then that I noticed a familiar sound in French: 'Prisonniers de guerre anglais'. Our guards were Frenchmen conscripted into the German Army! Anyway, they saved my nuts from being cracked.

The rest of the night was spent in the shelter and we ventured out again only when the all clear finally sounded. After being feasted with the usual coffee, bread and black pudding, we were herded yet again to the end of the platform, where we must have waited an hour for the next train. I couldn't see much evidence of the last night's bombings, although previously bombed and deserted buildings could be seen. Perhaps last night they had been after the harbour or factory area.

The same type of passenger train with hard seats jerked to a halt and in I piled, wondering where we were off to next. It was a slow train. On the way I noticed some very big fresh craters on either side of the railway. I counted twenty, each approximately 100 yards from the lines. Maybe it was the very high altitude bombing coupled with the intense flak that had put them off target. By 15.00 we had arrived at our final station and the guards were assuring us that we would be well looked after, with a good bed and Red Cross parcels. This made me feel better, for by now we were all weak through lack of proper food and medical attention.

There must have been another hour's wait at the station until an old Army-type lorry with solid tyres turned up. I couldn't care less at this stage, provided I didn't have to hobble on crutches. Before long I saw a large POW camp ahead, with its eight-foot high wire fencing and guards' platforms sticking up like sore thumbs all around. There was a collection of dingy looking huts dotting the interior. The lorry slowed at the gate and the senior guard jumped down to go through the handing over ceremony. Then the big wood and wire gates creaked open and the lorry jerked into the compound, where out we tumbled.

I was exhausted, and sweating as if I had just come out of a Turkish bath. My stump was throbbing. I stayed, lying on the ground where I landed, managing to support myself on one elbow, while the rest of the party sat, knelt or remained standing with the aid of their crutches. I didn't want a welcoming committee but wished that someone would show us where to go. One of the guards was busy having a chat and a laugh with his mate. Eventually he gave us the go-ahead and the party moved off slowly and wearily. I found myself left behind. I tried to get up but could not muster enough strength to make it. So I started crawling, dragging the crutches. I had only managed five or six yards when I heard voices and saw two pairs of gaitered boots. 'Come on me old mate', a voice said, 'we'll give you a lift'. On which, they lifted me with ease and carried me I don't know how far. I didn't even get a glimpse of their faces to say thanks. Sinking down on to a straw mattress, I just slept and slept for the next two days. When I awoke I found that I was in Stalag XIB in Saxony, along with a large number of other Airborne men.

It was not long before I contracted more complaints to add to my already sorry condition. Lice and bugs were in abundance in my hut. The nights were worst. The iron stove was stoked right up at night, and the heat was awful with all doors and windows shut tight. Urine buckets would fill to the brim in no time, making the stench nauseous. I went down with dysentery, pleurisy and scarlet fever, which together with my amputation meant that I did not feel all that good. If I had wanted to die I would have, but fortunately that didn't enter my head.

I had the pleasure of meeting Regimental Sergeant Major John Lord of our 3rd Para Battalion, whose parent regiment was the same as mine, the Grenadier Guards. RSM Lord became the camp disciplinarian. The Germans didn't like him because of his manner and first-class military bearing and our own men thought twice before offering any backchat. Even as a POW a serviceman comes under military protocol and is answerable for any misbehaviour. A few of the more cocky types didn't realise this at first but they had a big shock coming with RSM Lord. His dark piercing eyes penetrated your very inner private thoughts. He put the Germans to shame, with the slovenly way they paraded around the camp.

After a short time, promising news—I was told that I was going to be repatriated. I boarded yet another train. No sooner had we set off, than there was a terrific *whoosh* and the train stopped in the middle of nowhere. I could hear the guttural twang of German civilians as they ran hell for leather each side of the train to take cover from what must have been our own aircraft. Our guards just vamoosed and left us to it. Looking down to the track, I saw that it was much too high for me to jump with only one leg, though some of our party of eight jumped and took cover. I fouled my pants and don't know whether it was fright or the dysentery that was still with me. The planes returned. They were two rocket-firing RAF Typhoons, which specialized in ground attack. I recognized the sound as they got nearer. There was another *whoosh*, and then another, followed by an ear-splitting explosion. The carriage shook so violently that I thought we were going to topple over. As always in such attacks, it was over in no time and all was suddenly peaceful again.

People and guards began to trickle back; the front coach and engine had been hit they told us. We then had to wait about two hours before some German troops came and shifted the damaged engine. They must have used heavy lifting gear because both coach and engine lay neatly by the side of the track by the time we rolled by. It was dark when we came upon our last stop and I couldn't see much, except that it was a small station, suggesting a small town or village. Our guards did help us on this occasion and one offered me a shoulder to lean on in getting out of the carriage, which I was glad to accept.

This time things seemed a little more organised. I heard English-speaking voices, then a German. An English medic and two American medics loomed nearer. The Americans immediately handed around some cigarettes. Chesterfields they were. I enjoyed that first puff, as the English smokes I had were long gone. Someone had noticed them in Stalag XIB while I slept. They didn't pinch any but had reminded me of them when I awoke, and of the fact that no Red Cross parcels had arrived! We knew the Germans had been appropriating these, as the empty boxes were seen in the refuse area of the camp.

Now we had reached a snug little village called Meisburg, on the German side of the border with Belgium, near St Vith. Sympathetically, our new friends helped us on to a lorry, its wooden seats blanket-covered for added comfort. There were haversacks hanging on the sides, most likely with medical gear, as they bore a red cross on a white circle. There were even two folded English Army-style stretchers. These chaps had things running smoothly and they were very clean in dress and person. I could sense that our new abode was going to be just fine.

We did not travel far. The only Germans were at the checking-in office, run by a small party from the Pioneer Regiment, with a rottenführer section leader in charge of four shützen, or privates. I saw no guards. This was the village hall, being used to house wounded POWs. There were various out-houses turned into a cookhouse, shower, general medical stores, and, the biggest luxury of all, a flushing toilet. It was early evening. I heard a rumbling in the distance. 'Patton's Armoured Division', I was informed by a Yank from Ohio. 'They bin-a roamin' over tha hills, the last farv days'.

Our first job was to be cleaned up and we were taken in pairs to the shower. I was asked to remove all personal items from my pockets, as all clothing was to be cleaned and fumigated. 'Don't worry, you'll get everything back, good as new!' an English medic told me. 'Here, put this on.' It was a sort of cotton smock, which tied at the back and was just long enough to cover the knee. First, in came a great big American in the same garb, with forearms like tree branches. He lifted me bodily with the ease of Samson himself. Mind you, I was down from fourteen stone to just over eight since last September. On reaching the shower, his mate asked, 'Can you stand on one leg, bud?' 'Sure', I said. Samson had taken his smock off and proceeded to bathe me while Hercules steadied me. It was sheer heaven. After I had been rubbed down and smocked I was carried back to a most

152

luxurious bed with white sheets. God knows where they scrounged the sheets from, but trust the Yanks. There were approximately 40 wounded here, a mixture of English, French and American, with four American and two English orderlies. One of the walking wounded acted as cook, with others doing the menial tasks. They did not mind, though.

Pleasant surprises were not yet over: after English bully beef, poached eggs and German bread, with butter made from coal, we had tinned pears and cream. Then, to top it all, some Red Cross parcels had found their way here just before we arrived and we benefited from a generous share of the distribution, including chocolate, toothpaste and cigarettes, which were much sought after. The bulk of parcels consisted of tins of sausages, condensed milk, roast beef, and tins of steak and kidney pudding—one of the favourites. Dried fruit, boxes of cheese, a packet of Army-type biscuits, were much the same as they were at the beginning of the war, except that they were now 6 oz. packets instead of 4 oz. All the food was put into a pool to make up a respectable dish for everyone's taste. What a feast! I spent the next week in luxury after Stalag X1B.

Things began to liven up outside. The rumbling in the distance grew nearer and groups of bedraggled, weary-looking Germans plodded through the village, the wounded borne by horse and cart. Field guns were manhandled, the luxury of any motorised transport being afforded to senior officers only, who clearly wished to withdraw in as dignified a manner as possible, leaving the unteroffiziers to do all the donkey work along with the schützen, and suffer all the humiliation of being seen by their own countrymen. It was a pathetic sight, like a cutting from the First World War film archives.

As dawn approached, the throb of motorised transport and tanks was very near. You could hear the squeak of the tanks' wheels rubbing the caterpillar track, thirsty for lubrication, edging and shunting into position for the impending advance on the village. The American orderlies were jubilant. 'They're here, Limey. The Yanks are here!' exploded Hank. Anyone who could get up and walk, hop, or propel themselves in some way momentarily forgot their wounds and discomfort. They peered through cracks in doors, through windows. I could not see anything from my window, only the Nazi flag of the local garrison, hanging listless, like the enemy itself. Bill, one of the English medics, came dashing in not knowing which way to turn in his excitement: 'There's hundreds of tanks out there; bloody well hundreds of 'em!'

Sherman tanks of General Patton's Armoured Division had encircled the village in the early hours of the morning and were in a very advantageous position, as we were in the valley and they on the high ground. Every gun would have had its own selected target, with orders to open fire if fired upon. Thankfully, the tanks played a waiting game with a non-existent enemy, because unknown to the Americans the birds had flown.

An American scout car ventured cautiously towards the village. Unmolested, it reached the outskirts, scanning the buildings where white flags were protruding. No sign of the enemy. Still in view of the tanks on the hill, it became bolder and cruised gently into the village. Our makeshift hospital, with a painted red cross on the roof, must have been in view of the scout car now. All these goings-on were being shouted by one of the medics out in the passageway for the benefit of those like me who could not see for themselves.

The scout car came to a stop. Its occupants clutching their automatics at the ready: they must have spotted someone step carefully into view. That person was a medic with a Red Cross armband—Hank, the orderly from Ohio. He was about 100 yards from the scout car and they stealthily approached each other, Hank not wishing to be mistaken for a German ruse, those in the scout car not wishing to fall for any old trick. As they drew closer, the realization dawned that they were brothers. A wireless call was immediately sent to the tanks on the skyline and in minutes the village was alive to their rumble as they thundered on through, leaving an acrid smell of oil and exhaust fumes. I was almost home.

Epilogue

Thanks to the smooth running efficiency of the United States Army Air Force, on the 14th of April 1945 I was whisked in an ambulance to an airstrip somewhere in Germany, then emplaned in the type of aircraft I had come out in—a Dakota. Only this time I was lying down, not sitting. Passing over Belgium, we hit a rough storm, but landed OK in the south of England, where I finished up in Basingstoke Hospital.

I would never know the fate of many of my friends, though would meet up with a few in the years to come. The casualties in the Arnhem area alone were 8,000 Airborne killed, wounded, captured or missing, including Poles, plus more than 400 RAF pilots and crew. There were 750 Dutch civilians and underground fighters killed, at least 2,500 Germans, and in the following winter of 1944-5 some 200,000 Dutch died of starvation.

There has never been a full account of what really happened or went wrong at Arnhem. As portrayed later in the film of the same name, it was perhaps 'a bridge too far', but there was more to it than that. 'There has been no single performance by any unit that has more greatly impressed me or more highly excited admiration,' General Eisenhower had written to General Roy Urquhart, 1st Airborne Division Commander in 1944. We lost a lot to earn such praise.

It takes impeccable individuality and devotion to duty, irrespective of danger, no matter how great, to be awarded the Victoria Cross. No fewer than five VCs were awarded at Arnhem. They were to: RAF Flight Lieutenant David Lord DFC (posthumous); Lieutenant John Grayburn, 2nd Parachute Battalion (posthumous);

Captain Lionel Queripel, 10th Parachute Battalion (posthumous); Sergeant John Baskeyfield, 2nd South Staffords (posthumous); and Major Robert Cain, 2nd South Staffords. Many other medals for valour were earned also.

Several years later I visited the place of thinking, if you will, of that great man and founder of the Parachute Regiment, Winston Churchill: The War Rooms, situated far below ground at the Treasury Chambers in Westminster. The existence of this warren of rooms was a well-kept secret during the war years. The tour was fascinating; everything remained exactly as it had been back then. I sat in Churchill's chair, in front of me on the desk, printed in black on a card, the words of Queen Victoria: 'In this House we never speak of defeat.' In the toilet there was a red telephone, a direct line to President Roosevelt in Washington. In the visiting ministers room, I opened a book entitled 'World War Two' on the Sicily landings and saw a training shot of members of my 11th SAS Battalion. To the fore in the line-up were Harry Bance, Corporal Hutson, Jimmy Metcalfe and myself. Down here beneath Westminster, surrounded I am sure by a dedicated team, Churchill did his job extremely well. I would like to think that I did my best, alongside other Leopards, Lions and Tigers of the 1st Parachute Brigade.

***